Game Over

T0344644

Game Over

The Rise and Transformation
of a Harlem Hustler

Azie Faison

and Agyei Tyehimba

ATRIA BOOKS
New York   London   Toronto   Sydney

ATRIA BOOKS

A Division of Simon & Schuster, Inc.
1230 Avenue of the Americas
New York, NY 10020

First Atria Books trade paperback edition August 2007

ATRIA BOOKS and colophon are trademarks
of Simon & Schuster, Inc.

For information about special discounts for bulk
purchases, please contact Simon & Schuster Special Sales
at 1-800-456-6798 or business@simonandschuster.com.

Designed by C. Linda Dingler

Manufactured in the United States of America

10 9 8 7 6 5 4 3 2 1

Library of Congress Cataloging-in-Publication Data

Faison, Azie.
    Game over : the rise and transformation of a Harlem hustler / by
Azie Faison Jr. with Agyei Tyehimba.
        p. cm.
    Includes bibliographical references and index.
    1. Faison, Azie. 2. Drug dealers—New York (State)—New York—
Biography. 3. Drug traffic—New York (State)—New York. I. Tyehimba,
Agyei. II. Title.
    HV5805.F35A3 2007
    364.1'77092—dc22
    [B]   2007011447

ISBN-13: 978-0-7432-8231-4
ISBN-10:   0-7432-8231-0

Contents

Author's Note

*We wrestle not against flesh and blood, but against
principalities, against powers, against the rulers of
darkness of this world, against spiritual wickedness
in high places.*

—Ephesians 6:12

Thanks for your support. Seventy-five percent of the proceeds I earn from this book will go to a charity called Chariot 126, which benefits the seeds (children) of friends who died in the drug game. In reading this book, you are not only learning about my life, but you are also supporting people who lost family members to this foolish drug war.

You may have heard my story. Some learned about my story in the latest underground magazine, others from the movie *Paid in Full*, the documentary *Game Over*, or have heard major hip-hop artists shout me and my associates out in their songs. No matter what you heard, this book was not written to defend myself or to point fingers at anyone. It was not written for bragging rights or to compete in this vicious and foolish drug underworld.

I and some of my former associates are admired today by young people and hip-hop artists; many of them have patterned themselves after us. I regret that, since our activities led to death and destruction. Since then, in an effort to steer youth in the right direction, I've created a movie, a documentary, and this book to reverse the trends I and others set.

I'm writing *Game Over* to tell the truth about the world of narcotics trafficking in urban areas. Too many people admire the drug lifestyle, but that lifestyle and that world are based on falsehood and illusion. Despite popular music videos that glamorize street life, I can honestly say that almost everybody who was somebody in the drug world is dead, incarcerated, or working in collaboration with law enforcement.

I wish I never played this game. In writing this book, I had to recall the good and bad that happened to me and many others involved in the streets during the mid eighties and nineties in Harlem. As you read this book, I hope that you will make a decision to avoid the dirty game of drugs. There is no way out. If your thoughts are in the drug game, I write this book to change that direction of thought.

In this book you will experience the highlights in the criminal underworld: luxury cars, pretty ladies, money; in addition to betrayal, pain, and truth; to reveal that the drug "game" is not really a game at all . . . it is very serious. Those

Author's Note

who take the ugliness I describe in this book and continue to roll with it, glamorize it, or emulate it, are getting the wrong message. My message is captured in the book title: The game is over. The truth is in the youth. We must save the children.

—Azie Faison, Jr., 2007

Foreword

In 2002, I worked as an adjunct professor in the Ethnic Studies Department of the Borough of Manhattan Community College, located just a few blocks from the spot where the World Trade Center Towers once stood. I occasionally had talks with my students before or after class that often centered on current events and popular culture.

I respected the intelligence and passion of these students as I listened to their opinions about war, politics, racism, and the drug epidemic. I realized however, that their political consciousness was not reflective of the larger youth community. I often left these conversations feeling energized yet sad.

Young brothers and sisters had more technology and education than ever before in American history. Yet, black and Latino youth as a whole seemed more confused than ever. Many of these same youth are also more likely to be incarcerated, murdered, unemployed, and involved in the drug game than youth in prior generations. Never before had I seen young people embrace the most negative qualities and values of the ghetto and wear them as badges of pride.

Equally troubling was my observation that many public figures failed in their attempts to reach the youth. Young people view many politicians, preachers, and motivational speakers as irrelevant. Consequently, they turn a deaf ear to them. Rap music it seems, holds the attention of our youth because the lyrics speak to them through language and imagery that they can relate to.

On the other hand, too many of the rap artists in a position to influence the youth use their celebrity status to promote or glamorize the negative qualities that threaten to destroy our communities.

I spent time thinking about how to influence change in the mentality of our youth. I concluded that unlike their parents and grandparents, black youth in the twenty-first century have no national movement that inspires or motivates them. That movement, however—given our youth's disdain for traditional party politics, corporate America, and the church—must be spearheaded by people who connect with youth. Who had enough street credibility to earn their respect? Who was familiar with the drug game, hip-hop, and black street culture? Who survived the worst the streets had to offer, and lived to talk about it? Who had the political consciousness and spiritual foundation necessary to bring our youth from the darkness to the light? My questions were soon answered when I saw two films.

One day in the summer of 2002, I sat in a Harlem

apartment with a group of friends talking and relaxing. Someone brought bootleg copies of the movie *Paid in Full* and the documentary *Game Over*. I was interested in both films because I knew they dealt with the lives of Azie, Rich Porter, and Alpo. These three brothers were street legends in Harlem, and though I never met them, I constantly heard stories about them during my high school years.

As I watched both films, I knew that Azie Faison was a brother who could relate to youth and speak to them from experience. He had the street credibility so important to urban youth. He was a former cocaine dealer who became rich at a young age, he survived a vicious attack on his life, and he had formed his own rap group.

I saw from his documentary that he had a mission to expose people to the dangers of the drug game. I had the man for the job! I boldly announced to my friends that I would meet Azie one day, and that I would convince him to let me cowrite his life story.

Right after I saw the films, I spoke to Ms. Marie Brown about my book idea. Ms. Brown taught me creative writing on Saturdays at the Children's Art Carnival in Harlem; I was about nine years old then. Decades later, she was one of the most successful black literary agents in the country. (See how everything comes together?) Ms. Brown was interested, so my next goal was to find Azie.

Seven days later, while sitting in the Texas Star Diner in Harlem, I saw Azie! I approached him immediately, introducing myself as a fellow Harlemite and educator. I told him how much I liked his movie and documentary.

Then I pitched my idea to him: "How would you like to write your life story?" He seemed fairly interested, and he gave me his number. Roughly a year later, we began the process of interviewing and this book is the result. I never cease to be amazed by the power of positive thinking.

Sometimes the story behind the story is very interesting. Imagine the "coincidence" of me running into Azie one week after watching his films. Consider how a teacher from my past became my literary agent some twenty-eight years later.

It is important to appreciate how Azie's life and mine intersected. We shared Harlem stomping grounds. In fact, we grew up three blocks from each other. We are therefore familiar with many of the same Harlem landmarks, streets, and general culture.

Yet we chose two entirely different life paths. Azie is about four years my senior. He attended public schools in New York City, while I attended all private and parochial schools. When he began selling drugs, I was playing football at Cardinal Hayes High School. As he became a virtual kingpin in New York City, I—then known by my given birth name, Quentin Stith—was president of the Student African American Society at Syracuse University, organizing black students to challenge racism and create more opportunities for themselves. Azie faced the dangers of death and imprisonment, and I faced expulsion from school for being a political "troublemaker." He dropped out of school in the ninth grade while I went on to earn a master's degree from an ivy league university.

Throughout the process of writing this book, I couldn't

help thinking about how two black men from the same neighborhood could have led such different lives, yet be brought together to work on a project. We took different paths, but ultimately wound up at the same destination. To me, that story is almost as fascinating as the actual book.

Some may not understand the significance of a former drug dealer's life. Despite their reservations, Azie has become a street icon. *Paid in Full*, the movie based on his life, has become a cult classic. His self-produced documentary, *Game Over*, is tremendously popular and has inspired a slew of other independently produced and distributed street docudramas.

Perhaps Azie's story is so interesting because it involves all the elements of a classic gangster movie: drugs, money, sex, murder, revenge, and betrayal. Almost two decades after these events transpired, these qualities make people want to hear more, see more, and learn more about his story. Several prominent hip-hop magazines featured his story over the years. Largely due to the interview with Azie, the first issue of *F.E.D.S.* magazine sold like hotcakes. Several of today's hottest rap artists shout him out in their rhymes, and rapper Young Jeezy filmed a video to his song "Soul Survivor" depicting scenes reenacted from *Paid in Full*. A *Village Voice* article written in January of 2006 discussed how the crack epidemic of the 1980s influenced contemporary hip-hop. Three paragraphs of the story recall Azie's life as a drug dealer.

Do not be mistaken. This is no "guide for becoming a successful drug dealer." What makes this story transcend that of the typical street narrative is that Mr. Faison does not glamorize his past life. In fact, he wants to tell all who will listen how painful and destructive his life was. He openly criticizes his previous actions and actually cringes when referred to as a "kingpin." I can recall several times while working on this book when Azie pushed me to bring the "Game Over" chapter to a close. This chapter focuses on the murder and tragedy of the drug game, specifically of people close to him. I remember him telling me, "We got to bring this chapter to a close, brother . . . All that wickedness haunts me . . . I gotta get it out of my life."

To those who are skeptical about Azie's character or intentions, I offer this: He made a deliberate choice to end his criminal dealings and adopt the mission of reclaiming the lives of misguided youth. His former street credibility, added with his commitment to empower others, gives him an added ability to reach and connect with the downtrodden, disillusioned, and rejected.

We wrote this book to deliver a message of hope and positive change. I hope people refer to it for a realistic portrayal of street life and drug culture at the end of the twentieth century. I hope brothers and sisters in the 'hood—especially the hustlers—take Azie's revelations to heart. One book will not eliminate the drug game. However, one committed and informed voice can help to break the cycle of ignorance concerning drug culture in America's slums. This is my hope and my prayer.

—Agyei Tyehimba, 2007

1
Sugar Hill

"Open the safe, nigga! Open the fuckin' safe now, or I'm gonna kill everybody in this bitch! Hurry up, motherfucka..." That's the last thing he said before he hit me hard in the head with the butt of his gun, causing blood to flow into my eyes. Shaking with fear and numb from the pain, I tried to respond: "Look, man ... The blood is blinding me. I can't see! I don't have no money in the safe anyway. Just let everybody go ... I'll get you some money. They don't got nothin' to do with this."

I was on my knees, bent over, with blood pouring out of my head. I felt no pain; I was numb. This was my judgment day—payment for all my sins. God lost patience with me. Instead of listening, I ignored the Lord's warnings and turned my back on Him. I heard His voice throughout the years, but I wasn't sure it was Him. So there I was. My head was spinning, my heart was pounding, and my eyes were stinging from the sticky blood pouring into them.

Game Over

Stumbling around in pain, I managed to clear some blood from my eyes using my shirt. What I saw took my breath away: Five people, including my aunt and my best friend, were tied up in my aunt's bedroom. They were handcuffed and lying facedown, pleading for their lives. By nightfall, my aunt, her friend, and my best friend were pronounced dead. Two more people survived, but they sustained serious wounds. As for me, I took two shots to my head at point-blank range, and seven more: one to my neck, another in my shoulder, and the rest in my leg. I was shot nine times. I saw a bright light and my body felt like it was rising toward the light.

"We're losing him, we're losing him. He won't make it." The paramedics who rushed me to the hospital had no reason to believe I'd survive. In fact, I didn't survive . . . at least the old me didn't. On that day, the old me was killed so a new me could be reborn.

People who lived in New York City, especially Harlem, during the eighties and nineties regard me as a street legend. I made millions before I was old enough to vote, which allowed me to live a life most people only dream of living. Customized cars, fine women, property, and street respect were my way of life. I spent money at will and made it possible for many people in Harlem to eat and pay bills. Along with my associates, Rich Porter and "Alpo," I had no way of knowing that years down the road, our lifestyles would influence music, clothing, and even Hollywood.

How did I get so much money and influence at such a young age? I was a hustler . . . *yeah, I sold drugs*. I did my thing during the Pablo Escobar–Manuel Noriega–Oliver North era. Throughout the eighties and nineties, I probably sold enough cocaine to make it snow in New York City.

But anything built on negativity will eventually bring destruction to those who profit from it. In the end, we all paid a huge price for the fame and wealth we got by selling drugs. The drug game forced me to experience things that changed my life forever.

I was born in a Bronx hospital on November 10, 1964. I lived the first six years of my life between 165th and 167th Streets and Clay Avenue. We lived in a poor neighborhood, and like many other families on the block, we received public assistance, or welfare.

Many people like to say, "Even though we were poor, I never knew we were poor." I think people say that to show respect to their parents for trying to make ends meet. My parents did the best they could, given our situation. Poverty, like wealth, is something that is both hard to hide and hard to deny. I couldn't escape the reality that my family was poor. Everything from where we lived to how we lived, reminded us we were poor.

I had seven brothers and sisters: Wanda was the oldest, then came Kevin, Robin, Rosalyn (also known as "Pie"), me, Julie, Ingrid, and Wayne. Out of my sisters, Robin was my favorite because she knew how to mind her business and she knew plenty of street cats who made big money growing up.

I'll never forget when Wanda ran away from home to be with her boyfriend at the time. She returned months later . . . and she was pregnant! My mother greeted her with open arms. I guess she was just happy to have her firstborn back home.

My little sister Ingrid was my little baby girl. I was proud of her because she graduated from A. Phillip Randolph High School, located on the City College campus, and eventually did a year of college. By Ingrid's senior year in high school, I told her that when she graduated I would buy her a car. I was about twenty-one years old at the time, and I kept my promise.

My brother Kevin graduated from John F. Kennedy High School, and entered the United States Marine Corps. He only stayed for a couple of months before he received a dishonorable discharge. I believe it had something to do with him smoking weed.

Wayne was the baby of the family, and like most babies, he was spoiled. He never wanted for anything. When I got into the game and had major money, I bought Wayne and my nephew hot dirt bikes one Christmas. They became the envy of the block, since most kids barely had regular bikes at the time.

My sister Pie was something else. At Stitt Junior High, she won the beauty pageant, which made her and me very popular in the school. Julie was always very quiet and reserved. She stayed to herself or under my mother.

Things were so tight back then that nine of us lived in a one-bedroom apartment. My parents occupied the bedroom, and we slept in the living room on a pullout couch or the floor.

To be fair, we took turns sleeping on the couch. Everyone hated the floor because you usually woke up with a permanent crick in your neck and a sore back. On the nights I had the floor, I used pillows to cushion myself. It wasn't comfortable, but we didn't have a choice so we made the best of it. Poverty robs you of options.

Poverty also influences your decisions. For example, not having much money actually motivated us to attend school every day (although we didn't always *stay* in school all day). We appreciated school not just for the lessons, or the friendships we made, but because it provided us with two hot meals daily. We all went to school early to get breakfast, and *never* missed lunch. Dinner was the only meal we had at home during the week, and usually this consisted of a bologna or ham sandwich and some juice or milk.

My mother, Margaret Rogers, was a native New Yorker. She met my father when she was twenty years old; he was forty. I figure she wanted to get with an older man who could provide her with a good quality of life.

Short, fair-skinned, and heavyset, my mother was a housewife who wanted to enjoy life's finer things, having grown up poor herself. Unfortunately, my father's salary could not support her desires. As a result, she constantly reminded my father of how broke we were.

My mother was always a great cook. She made huge feasts for the holidays, and we couldn't wait to get our hands on her apple cobbler and smothered turkey wings. I liked everything she cooked with the exception of chitlins—the entire house smelled like shit whenever she prepared them. She believed everyone had the right to eat and eat well. In fact, people would often knock on our door, and my mother would make them plates with no hesitation.

My father, Azie Faison, Sr., was born and raised in Fort Lauderdale, Florida. He stood about five feet nine and wasn't very large, but he carried himself like a giant. He was dark-skinned with strong, proud facial features. He had jet-black hair like a Native American and honest, penetrating eyes that looked right through you.

My mother taught me the importance of making money. My father, on the other hand, taught me how to be a man. He wasn't just *a* man; he was *the* man. He was the most humble and reliable person I've ever known. He moved furniture for a living so he didn't make a lot of money. But he worked hard to support our household. Unlike many men at the time, he didn't smoke, drink, gamble, chase women, or maintain a fancy wardrobe.

My father didn't try to be something he wasn't and he didn't change for anybody. I remember times my mother would have some girlfriends over at the house, laughing and gossiping. My father would sit quietly in his chair watching television. Once they left, my father would mutter, "Thank God. Now I can relax and have my space." Privacy and humility were important to him. I never remember anyone saying a bad word about him.

When I got involved with the drug game, my father was the only family member who didn't ask me for money or presents. He told me he "wanted nothing to do with my blood money."

It wasn't until I began selling coke, around 1983, that

I had huge knots of cash. I felt like I was *the man* because I brought in more money in a week than my father did in a year. Cocaine sales made me the main breadwinner in the house. I paid the rent, bought food and items for the apartment, and gave my mother rolls of money whenever she needed it. I figured that since I took care of the home, nobody could tell me shit.

And it seemed like everybody in the house respected my authority—everybody except my father. My money didn't mean shit to him. He refused my money and demanded my mother do the same (although my mom had no problems accepting it when he wasn't around). As far as he was concerned, he was the man of the house, and still had the authority to regulate his children. He proved that one day when he came into my room and caught me bagging up some coke. I had shit everywhere: a huge mound of coke, baggies, a scale, and hundreds of little vials.

"What's this? What are you doing in my house?" he asked. "You get involved with those drugs and you're gonna pay," he warned. "And if you are selling that poison, I don't want nothing to do with you until you stop."

I ignored every word and didn't even reply. In my ignorance (and arrogance) I shut him down and shrugged him off. That was the turning point in our relationship. For the first time, I didn't yield to his authority. He shook his head in disappointment and left. True to his word, he stopped speaking to me from that day until I got shot years later.

People out for your money will do and say shit to keep your money rolling in. Those who really love you will try to point you in the right direction and rock the boat no matter how you react. My father took the right stand despite the fact that his own wife and children did the opposite. For that, he always got my maximum respect.

Even when I learned that he was not my biological father, I still saw him as my dad. I'll never forget when my sister came to my job at the cleaners with a tall cat claiming he was my "real" father. I couldn't front, I looked just like the dude. I told him without blinking or stuttering: "Look, man, nice meeting you, but you ain't my father. My father is in the house right now."

"But, Azie, this is our fa—"

"Nah, sis," I interrupted. "That's *your* father. My father is in the house handling his business like he's done all my life."

I guess the brother didn't want to fight a losing battle, so he nodded to me with a sour look on his face and left with my sister. That was the first and last time I saw my biological father. My sisters stayed in touch with him, and sometimes got money and presents from him. I didn't bother. The man I was named after was in my life since the day I was born.

There are two types of women. Those who recognize the qualities a man brings to the table, like being honest and hardworking, and those who judge a man by his finances. My mother was the second type of woman. When she wasn't complaining about what we didn't have, she was telling us to get jobs to help support the house.

My mother received welfare, which helped us to pay rent and purchase food and clothes for our family. Receiving welfare brought certain humiliating requirements or conditions. One condition was that my father had to leave the house whenever a welfare worker came by. To qualify for the benefits, we had to give them the impression that our father did not live with us. Had my father been present, we would lose our welfare benefits because of the money he made.

My mother often warned us not to miss school. Absences might cause a welfare worker to visit our home for what they called a "face-to-face" meeting with my mother. She was scared to death of these meetings, because they might jeopardize her welfare payments. I guess the worker could also determine that a parent was negligent in raising their children, and possibly have the children separated from their parents.

Television allowed me to forget some of my problems, laugh, and escape to a fantasy world. Unlike real life, everything on television seemed to work out right.

During the 1970s, shows centered on black characters began flooding our televisions. Network executives finally realized that black people had lives worth exploring too. Or maybe they saw that black people made up a market they needed to take advantage of. I never missed an episode of *Good Times*, *The Flip Wilson Show*, *Sanford and Son*, *The Jacksons* variety show, *The Richard Pryor Show*, *What's Happening!!* or *The Jeffersons*.

I really liked *Good Times*; I think many children in the 'hood did. The show gave viewers a glimpse into the lives of a poor family living in a Chicago housing project. Episodes explored a number of topics children like me could relate to, like unemployment, school bullying, and peer pressure. The characters on the show appealed to us, because in looking at J.J., Michael, or Thelma, we saw people we knew in our own families or neighborhoods. We all knew a Willona-type character, a female friend of the mother who often came over to gossip: What urban 'hood didn't have a character like Lenny, who sold everything you could think of at discount prices? Many of us could relate to a strong mother figure like Florida Evans or a hardworking dad like James who did what he could to "bring home the bacon."

Our parents sometimes let us have company, and we watched some of these TV shows together. Times like that were embarrassing because our television set was busted. The dial was always broken, so we could only turn the channel by sticking a fork into the TV. Whenever someone turned the channel with that fork, my friends would get on my case the next day in school. The big joke among my friends was that watching television at my house was like having a "TV dinner."

You can learn about a society or culture by checking out their popular television shows. When I was growing up, most shows were about families, and having good clean fun. Things weren't that graphic back then. The most you saw was a little kissing. You never heard inappropriate words. Now, people can say "ass" and "bitch" on network shows. I guess television reflects the values of society.

Of course, television wasn't our only form of entertainment. Every kid in the 'hood played puff basketball. You had a small Nerf basketball—a soft, spongy little ball—

and a little hoop that any kid could reach. Nerf basket-
balls were cool because you could hit things with them
without breaking anything.

My brothers and sisters and I loved to dance. We tried
to imitate the Jackson Five by dancing and lip-synching
in the mirror. Or sometimes we acted out episodes of the
Little Rascals. We would sing their songs and try to speak
like them. As a last-ditch effort at amusing myself, I loved
to scare my sisters at night. I would hide in their bed or
behind the curtain, and jump out once they fell asleep.

We also played the typical childhood games like hide-
and-seek, musical chairs, Simon says, and different card
games. Besides helping us have fun, these games helped
develop our physical fitness and social skills.

I think most kids love to play fight, and my family was
no different. I loved to wrestle with my brothers and sisters. To win the match, you had to pin the person down
and count to three before they got up. One time, my
mother bought me and my brother some boxing gloves,
and we got busy. My brother Kev and I used to battle like
Muhammad Ali and Joe Frazier all the time, and he usually whipped my ass.

Sometimes our games got too serious. One day Kevin
punched me hard in the stomach and knocked the wind
out of me. I felt like I was about to die, but I recovered
and I challenged him to a rematch. I tried to take his head
off. We had to quit before things went too far.

When the movie *Star Wars* came out, Kev and I
pretended we were Darth Vader and Luke Skywalker. We
used curtain rods for light sabers. I was Luke Skywalker,

the good guy. After saying "May the force be with you," I proceeded to light his ass up. We had a good battle going until I accidentally poked him in the eye. Kev ran into my sister Wanda's room crying with a bloody eye. "Look what Junior did to me! Look at my eye!" Anybody who grew up with siblings knows that the older sister tries to police shit in the house when the parents are gone, and my sister Wanda was no different: "Look what you did! Why did you do that?"

My brother made his case and had the evidence to prove it. He was the prosecutor and my sister was the judge. I tried my best to give a good defense.

"We were playing. He was hitting me too. I didn't do it on purpose. He ran into it." Wanda wasn't having it. She whipped my ass, and then told my mother. My mother whipped my ass, then told my father when he returned from work. Then my father whipped my ass.

Kev wasn't satisfied. He wanted me to get more punishment. While my father was beating me, Kev ran into the room crying again (hours after the shit happened) talking about how much his eye still hurt. Next thing I knew, my mother, father, and sister started whipping my ass at the same time. I got jumped by my own family!

One thing I hated about growing up with brothers and sisters was favoritism. In big families, it always seems like one child gets more love from the parents than the rest. In my family, when we were young, Kevin was the favorite. He was a pretty-boy type with soft, curly hair. He got fewer beatings than anybody else, and always got better presents than I did.

For example, my mother bought me pants from Alexander's department store. Alexander's was a store where you could purchase just about anything for a low price. Kev, on the other hand, got brand-name stuff. I got no-name sneakers—we called these cheap sneakers "skips." Kev got brand-name sneakers like Pro-Keds.

Kev and I had different fathers. I believe that my mom was truly in love with Kev's father, and never really got over him. Every time she looked at Kevin, she saw his father and probably thought about the good times they shared. Maybe this explains why she always took good care of him. I think parents should be careful not to play favorites. No child should grow up feeling better or less than anyone else in the house. I felt like my mother loved him more than she did me; this made me feel like I didn't matter.

Sometimes the drama of real life drowns out the laughter or sense of escape provided by television shows. Around the time I was five years old, in the winter of 1970, I had my first brush with death. My brothers and sisters were at school. My little sister Julie, who was about three years old at the time, was at home with me and our mother. My mother was cooking when she had to suddenly run out.

"Azie, I got to go. Stay here and I'll be back. Keep an eye on your little sister. Don't leave this house, do you understand?"

"Yes, mama."

She bolted out the door and locked it. Soon I began to smell smoke, so I went in the kitchen to investigate. The thick smoke made me cough and made my eyes water.

Game Over

Our kitchen was on fire! I grabbed Julie and tried to open the front door, but it locked from the outside. I ran to the window but it was also locked and wouldn't budge. I started to panic and banged on the window. I was scared to death. I thought we were going to die. I felt hopeless and with nowhere to turn.

No one heard my cries for help, and smoke continued to fill the house. I was in shock and I felt numb. At five years of age, I was not mature enough to be responsible for myself, let alone my little sister Julie. No one had ever told me what to do in case of an emergency in the home. Not knowing what to do, I looked up to the sun and I prayed: "Please, God, help us." Thank God, my father arrived just in the nick of time and unlocked the door.

"Margaret . . . Margaret," he screamed, calling for my mother.

"Daddy, over here by the window," I said.

He rushed over and picked us up, asking, "Where's your mother?" He was visibly upset.

"I don't know . . . she left," I replied, still coughing from the smoke.

He rushed us downstairs to safety and took us across the street in the freezing cold. He wrapped us in his coat and we watched as our entire building burned down. Julie was crying and the smoke aggravated her asthma. I was dazed. All I could think was "Where do we go from here?" Everything we had was gone almost in the blink of an eye.

I often think about that day, and how strange my mother acted. I never had the nerve to ask her directly about that incident. I guess it brings back some painful memories. The fire made us temporarily homeless. We actually moved to a shelter. I don't remember much about the shelter, but I was sure glad the social workers found us a place in Harlem a few months after the fire.

To me, Harlem is the most powerful 'hood in the world: the Mecca. It's where all the trends begin, where young kids learn their walk, their slang, and their 'hood fashion. We moved to the famous Sugar Hill section of Harlem, a spot I'm very proud of. Sugar Hill runs from Edgecombe Avenue to Amsterdam Avenue and from 145th Street to 155th Street. If you lived in Sugar Hill during the first half of the twentieth century, it was a sign that "life was sweet" or that you had made it.

Many rich and successful blacks lived in the area from 1920 to 1950. The list includes such notables as Adam Clayton Powell, Jr., Paul Robeson, Madame C. J. Walker, Langston Hughes, W.E.B. DuBois, Roy Wilkins, Thurgood Marshall, Marcus Garvey, James Baldwin, Zora Neale Hurston, and Duke Ellington.

In *The Autobiography of Malcolm X*, brother Malcolm described how he adopted Harlem as his hometown. An older brother I know named Charles told me that during Malcolm's criminal days, Malcolm did much of his dirt in Sugar Hill. Later, as a Nation of Islam minister, he worked his old turf, this time holding rallies and organizing meetings.

Harlem also had its share of criminal legends. These were flamboyant characters who spent big money, dressed stylishly, and became rich in the criminal underworld.

Game Over

The movie *Hoodlum*, starring and produced by Laurence Fishburne, explored the life of Ellsworth "Bumpy" Johnson, a legendary numbers banker in Harlem for over three decades.

The infamous Leroy "Nikki" Barnes established his heroin empire in Harlem, and made tons of money throughout the sixties and seventies. Harlem's reputation—the good and bad—made it known as the place where people hustled hard, made tons of money, and did things with flava and style.

Sometime in the spring of 1970, my family moved into 723 St. Nicholas Avenue, located on the corner of West 146th Street. The area changed over the years, but back then, Harlem had the feeling of a close-knit community. Older neighbors in the 'hood would discipline you for doing something bad, and then tell your parents so they could beat your ass too.

Compared to our old neighborhood in the Bronx, this part of Harlem had it going on. The people seemed to make more money and be more successful. The buildings even looked nicer than the ones in the Bronx.

I attended elementary school at P.S. 186, located on 145th Street between Amsterdam and Broadway. I completed first through fourth grades there, until the school closed in 1975 due to its dilapidated and unsafe condition. The building remains, but has stood idle and in disrepair for many years.

A new elementary school, P.S. 153 at 146th and Amsterdam, opened in its place. I entered the school for fifth grade. Our entire first year at 153 was spent moving all the materials from P.S. 186 to the new site. We didn't do any actual schoolwork during that whole year. I remember all of us carrying books from one school to the other, every day. Instead of paying us, the Board of Education promoted us to sixth grade even though we really hadn't learned anything.

I loved doing magic tricks. Ms. Frazier, my fifth grade teacher, would let me stand up and do tricks during the last fifteen minutes of class, if everyone behaved every day. I really looked forward to the time when Ms. Frazier would give me the stage to "do my thing."

"If y'all act right today, I'll let Azie do one of his famous magic tricks," she'd say.

This gimmick usually worked because the students loved my tricks and Ms. Frazier liked having an orderly class. You name the magic trick and I did it. I had card tricks, could turn one ball into three, and could pour water into newspaper shaped into a cone, then make the water vanish. I even knew how to make a coin disappear into thin air.

A few years later, magic got me into my first bit of trouble with the law. I had this brand-new book of tricks that I carried everywhere. I was coming home from junior high school one day, waiting in the train station reading my trick book. A dude I knew from school named Orlando ran up, snatched the book from me, and tossed it on the train tracks.

It was like somebody flipped on my "crazy" switch. I tossed his ass on the train tracks and wouldn't let him up until he gave my book back. The police saw the whole thing, so they snatched both of us and called our parents. My mother came to the precinct to get me, and she was furious.

"Boy, you and that other boy could've got hit by a train . . . and for what, a stupid book?" Parents have a way of mentioning the worst case scenario to make a point. That scenario for her was us getting killed by an oncoming train. For me, it was letting some other kid ruin an important possession of mine without me kicking his ass. My concerns reflected typical street thinking: Protecting one's property or upholding one's respect was more important than issues of life or death.

There were times during my childhood when I experienced spiritual moments I didn't fully understand at the time. When I was nine years old, to help make ends meet I bagged groceries for Ms. Evelyn after school every day at a local supermarket on 145th and Broadway called the Food Pageant. I made my little two or three dollars on weeknights, and ten dollars or so on the weekends. But one night I'll never forget. It was Halloween Eve. I usually packed bags until Ms. Evelyn got off work, which was usually nine o'clock. This night I wanted to leave early, at 7:30 p.m.; I desperately wanted to get home to watch *It's the Great Pumpkin, Charlie Brown.*

I asked Ms. Evelyn for permission to leave early. Since the store wasn't busy, she said, "No problem, Azie. I can take it from here. See you tomorrow."

I left work and ran to the store to pick up some goodies. I ran home just in time to see my sisters and brothers gathered around the television to watch the show.

I handed out my goodies. My mother entered the living room from her bedroom saying, "Junior, before you get comfortable, run to the store and get a loaf of bread so I can make y'all some sandwiches before you go to bed."

I jumped up and ran out the house as quick as possible, trying to outrun time itself so I could make it back to catch the beginning of the show. I rushed to the store, grabbed the loaf of bread, paid, and ran out of the store.

All I could remember is hearing Mr. Stokes, the storeowner, saying, "Slow down, boy. What's the hurry?"

When I left the store, it was like I was in another time zone, or a desert. I looked around, scared to death. All the buildings were gone, along with the store I'd just left. There were no cars or anything. All I saw was the sun beaming brighter than it ever did before. Sand covered the streets. I saw a mirage of my building about a mile away. I started running toward it, fast as I could, in fear.

As I ran, every footstep I took, I heard a loud footstep behind me. It seemed like the faster I ran, the faster it ran. It made me stop in my tracks to see what was behind me. I turned around, only to see the sun now hovering over me in the shape of a cross with a loop on top. I'd never seen anything like it before. I turned and began running faster. The footsteps behind me grew louder and louder. I made it to my building and went inside, and suddenly, the moment I entered the building, all that took place left my mind as if it never happened. I went to my apartment door and rung the doorbell. My mother, very upset, began yelling and cursing at me.

Game Over

"Where the fuck you been at? I'm gonna beat your ass if you don't tell me where you're coming from."

Confused, I said, "Come on, Mom, stop playing. I'm gonna miss the show."

My mother replied by saying, "Boy, do you know what time it is? It's after eleven o'clock. I had to send your brothers and sisters outside without anything to eat. I sent them to find you, but they said they couldn't find you anywhere."

Still confused, I said, "Come on, Mom. I went to the store and came right back. Look," I said as I showed her the bread I bought.

She snatched the bread, then grabbed me and pushed me in the room, telling me to go to sleep.

"Your father is gonna whip your ass when he comes home from work. This ain't like you, Junior. I sent you to the store hours ago." She cried as she walked back to her bedroom.

I sat on my bed in the room, in deep thought. I tried my best to do the right thing. Out of all my brothers and sisters, only I worked hard to help support our household. I packed bags and delivered papers. I gave my mother seventy-five cents of every dollar I made. "Why me, God?"

No sooner than I asked, there was a knock on my window. I moved the curtain back only to see the sun in the shape of a strange cross again. Scared to death, I jumped back into bed and pulled the covers over myself. Soon afterward, my father entered my room shaking me.

"Get up! It's time for school. What, you gonna sleep all day 'cause you was hanging out all night?"

I'm thinking, "Wow, I just laid down."

I was too young to understand what took place at that time. Looking back, I believe it was God's way of telling me he had a plan for my life, a plan I couldn't run away from. I didn't fully understand that plan until 1987. And it wasn't until years later that I realized the strange cross was an ankh, the Egyptian symbol of eternal life.

School 2 Daze

The year was **1976**. It was America's two hundredth birthday and everyone seemed to be concerned with celebrating the bicentennial. I remember the colorful parades, fireworks, "God Bless America" T-shirts, cookouts, and procession of majestic ships sailing along the Hudson River. The significance of America's bicentennial was lost on me, though. By the time I got to Edward Stitt Junior High School, my main concern was my appearance.

I wanted to dress nice, but didn't have the money. Yet, I still managed to wear the latest clothes out. How? I worked at the cleaners. If a customer brought in clothes that fit me and were stylish, those clothes became mine for a day. I would wear the clothes the next day, and walk through school feeling important as I caught looks of admiration from other students. Later that afternoon, I would bring the clothes back to the cleaners and put them back into the plastic like new. By the time the customer picked up the clothes, they would never know someone had worn them! Using this little scheme, my temporary wardrobe included mock necks, bell-bottom Levi's jeans, the pinstriped overalls we called "farmers," trench coats, and velour sweaters . . . I had the works.

It was also during my time at Stitt that school became less interesting for me. I began to cut class. My boys and I would often leave the building to play basketball at a court right by school on 168th Street and Audubon Avenue. The courts were popular because they were "biddies," meaning the hoops were a lot lower than regulation baskets. The average cat in school could dunk on a biddy basket, so we would sometimes spend the whole school day acting out our fantasies of playing professional ball.

One day when we were ballin' with some Dominican cats, my boy shot me a nice behind-the-back pass. When I jumped up to dunk, I hit my head hard on the backboard and busted my head wide open!

Luckily, Columbia Presbyterian Hospital was right across the street. I needed stitches, but the doctors refused to do any work on me until a parent or legal guardian came. My mother soon arrived and I got stitches and a good ass-whipping when we got home.

One day in eighth grade, my friend Stanley and I cut class. We chilled out in the hallway and bumped right into the principal, Mr. Tippet. Talk about bad luck! Mr. Tippet was black, somewhere in his early forties, and had a big Afro. He always wore nice suits and ties, and he definitely did not play! Most of us thought he was mean.

Mr. Tippet dragged us into his office and called our parents. It was funny because Stanley's mother got there so fast, it seemed like she was there before Mr. Tippet hung up the phone. When Stanley's mom arrived, she started beating the living shit out of Stan. "Didn't I tell you about hanging out with Azie? He's gonna get you in a world of trouble!"

Since Mr. Tippet couldn't reach my mother, and since I couldn't go until he spoke to her, I stayed in his office for about three hours. You know how you look at the clock and it seems to move slower than usual? That's how I felt. I was bored to death sitting in his office all day.

To make matters worse, the principal started doing things to fuck with me. He would write something down on a piece of paper, then ball it up and toss it in the garbage. Every time he missed, he'd tell me to pick it up and throw it out. I know he was missing on purpose. Meanwhile I was thinking, "I'm not his maid; he needs to pick his own shit up."

At some point, Mr. Tippet walked by and tripped over my foot. He thought I tripped him on purpose.

"You think that's funny, young man?"

"Mr. Tippet, I didn't mean to—"

"Don't lie to me, Mr. Faison. We'll see how you like it when you can't participate in graduation or go to the prom, *and* get suspended for the next two weeks."

No matter what I said, Mr. Tippet wouldn't believe me. He kept his word. I missed graduation and the prom, all because the principal tripped over my foot.

I looked forward to attending the prom and my graduation, and at first I was disappointed with Mr. Tippet's decision. Most students don't like to feel left out of events like that, but I knew my family couldn't afford to buy me a good suit or pair of shoes anyway. I felt somewhat relieved that I couldn't go, because it would spare me the embarrassment of showing up looking busted. My mother scraped some money together and took me to see the movie *Cooley High* on graduation day.

Ask any junior high school student and they'll tell you how difficult life can be during those years. You want more independence, your body is changing, you're interested in girls but don't know how to approach them, and you have to contend with bullies and troublemakers.

There was this bully I had to deal with. Everybody was scared of him because he was taller and heavier than the average eighth grader. In fact he was much bigger than the average student. He looked like he lifted weights, and he took advantage of this fact by fucking with everybody. We were in the same class, and I had a feeling that one day we were gonna bump heads.

One day after school I was standing outside waiting for the bus. The bully came up from nowhere, grabbed my book bag, and threw it in the street. I punched him in the stomach as hard as I could, then took off. A few of my other classmates saw the whole thing, and started spreading rumors about how I punched this cat in the stomach and got away with it.

The next day everybody in school was talking about what happened. "Yo, Azie gonna fight after school." This cat kept looking at me like he was gonna kill me. I did what anybody would do. I left school early! I talked to a guy who dated my sister Robin, and he gave me advice:

"What school you go to, shorty?"

"Stitt."

"Yo, don't even worry about it. When the bell rings, just walk out real slow. I'm gonna bring some dudes through."

I went back to school feeling like nothing could touch me. People kept asking me if I was going to fight. "Hell yeah, I'm gonna fight. Ain't nobody scared of him," I would reply, with a false sense of confidence.

"You talking all that shit now, nigga. Just wait till the bell rings," the bully replied once word got back to him.

When we got out of school, I walked slowly, just like I was told. I was confident that I had shit under control. I figured the older dudes would be there to make sure my enemy didn't use a weapon or try to get me jumped. They had my back.

After a while I didn't see my sister's boyfriend or his boys so I started to get a little nervous. "Where are these cats?" I thought. My adversary began walking toward me talking shit. Hundreds of students followed behind us waiting to see the big showdown. We took off our coats and faced each other, ready to rumble. I swung and caught him hard in the face. The crowd went wild as he rushed me and threw me in a headlock.

Next thing I knew, four or five cats came forward and started pounding the guy. Those dudes punched him in the face, threw him to the ground, and began stomping the shit out of him. One of the cats grabbed me and said,

"You see him? Don't you ever fuck with Azie again, or it's gonna be worse. He's family. He don't fuck with you, so don't fuck with him."

I doubt he was able to hear the warning, because he was in a daze. Those boys beat him so bad he had to be hospitalized.

After the beat-down, I had "juice." The word in school was that "you better not fuck with Azie or you gonna get your ass kicked." I got instant respect in school, and even got more attention from the girls. And the cat *never* fucked with me again. As a matter of fact, we became real cool after that.

My 3 Hood

I was bored with most of my classes in junior high, but the one class I did like was social studies. The credit for that went to my teacher, Mr. Marshall. Mr. Marshall was a tall, light-skinned brother. He carried himself with a sense of pride and seriousness, kind of like Malcolm X. He taught us things we couldn't find in the history books.

Mr. Marshall taught us about *our* history. He taught us that all black people came from Africa and that we had advanced civilizations long before we were enslaved. The thing he stressed most was self-identity: We should know ourselves and where we came from. This was my first exposure to black history and cultural empowerment. Years later, after I stopped hustling and began reading deeply, Mr. Marshall's lessons came back into focus.

We gave other teachers hell, but were attentive in Mr. Marshall's class because he made us believe we could succeed and make a better life for ourselves. He also had a reputation for being a mean and no-nonsense type of teacher. If he saw you flirting in class he would quickly remind you that "you are here to learn, not go on dates." And when you violated his rules, he popped you on the hand with a ruler. These days, a teacher would lose their job and possibly their life if they dared to hit a kid.

We had what was called a G.O. (General Organization) card, and for three dollars, it was your pass to all the after-school events. One of these events was a tournament called "Around the World," a basketball game where you had to shoot the ball from every point around the key on the court. You couldn't move on to the next part of the key until you hit your shot. It was like a relay race. One person on the team had to make their shots around the key before the next person on their team could start. Once everyone on the team went around the key, they won.

I entered the tournament in eighth grade. We made it to the finals, but were on our way to losing. Our opponents had one last man who was about four places ahead of me. In order to win, I would have to hit every shot. The crowd started cheering for me, "Azie! Azie!" Meanwhile, my opponent just needed to make two more baskets to finish us off.

I made my first two shots without touching the rim, *swish!* Then I hit my next two shots, *swish!* Luckily for me, the other dude just couldn't make his last baseline shot. I caught up to him, and the pressure was on. Whoever made this last shot won the tournament and left with the trophy. He shot and missed. I set up, took my time, jumped, and shot the ball. The crowd chanted, "Azie, Azie, Azie." It was like everything was in slow motion. The ball went high in the air and looked like it would take forever to come down. But when it did . . . *swish!* Nothing but net, or as they say now, "All water!"

I made all of my shots, and the crowd went crazy. I brought us back. We won the tournament and left the gym with a hot trophy. Stitt Junior High School! It was the best feeling in the world.

When I scored that winning basket in my school tournament and heard the crowd go crazy I felt like a hero. I could just imagine how the real superstars felt when they made a winning play in front of a national audience.

This is why I believe it's important for youth to get involved in sports. You learn teamwork, and develop a sense of pride. Plus, playing real games might prevent youth from getting caught up in illegal games. It is important to *win* in something that really counts.

Every day I sat in school, I couldn't wait for the last bell to ring. A regular day for me meant I would rush to 146th Street and St. Nick to hook up with my boys. We would sneak into Colonial pool on 145th Street and Bradhurst Avenue. It was the only large outdoor pool in the neighborhood, and part of the Jackie Robinson Parks and Recreation Center. In the spring and fall seasons, the pool had no water so we played baseball in the empty pool and used metal garbage can tops for bases.

When we got tired of baseball, we'd play two-hand touch football on 146th Street between Covent and St. Nick. We marked end zones by using manhole covers in the street. Stoopball was another favorite sport of ours, and we broke a lot of windows in the process of playing.

The girls had their street games too. My sisters got together with their friends to jump rope or play hopscotch. All of us were young and innocent.

There was mad love on the streets, and I remember a lot of good times. I can never forget Miss Kimble, who was a wonderful woman, and a true queen. She helped youth get summer jobs, gave block parties, and ran a free lunch program. Her block parties were always off the hook and mad crowded. We had all types of free food at her parties: cheeseburgers, franks, you name it.

DJ Randy Ran spun the records, and Kurtis Blow would be there controlling the mic. Songs like "Good Times" and "Heartbeat" played, and tons of kids did the latest dances like the Spank and the Hustle. Sometimes they even set up a portable pool on the block or a huge movie screen.

The adults drank liquor hidden in paper bags and smoked weed wrapped in Bambu paper. Back in the seventies, that happened on the regular. Those parties were so much fun that we never wanted to leave, and the police would have to come shut those parties down and send everybody home.

We were all one big family. You really didn't have to leave the community for anything. And, there were a whole bunch of community people whom I'll always remember.

Old-timers like Mr. Wiz protected the neighborhood, so we always felt safe. Mr. Wiz was a black man with green eyes. At one time, he was Bumpy Johnson's right hand man. He once showed me a platinum pinky ring given to him by the Mafia boss Lucky Luciano. Boy, did he have some war stories! I learned a lot about how the streets operated from people like Mr. Wiz.

He was no one to fuck with. It was common knowledge that he never left home without his gun on his waist, and would not hesistate to use it if necessary. One day while he did lookout duty for Bumpy, a man attempted to rob the gambling spot. As he pulled out his sawed-off shotgun, he ran right into Mr. Wiz's .45 caliber. Mr. Wiz blew him away then sat right down on the steps to read his newspaper until the police arrived.

I saw Mr. Wiz many years later. I greeted him and asked how things were going. In typical fashion he replied, "As long as arthritis don't hit my trigger finger I'm fine." He's an old man now, but still a player.

By 1979, I attended George Washington High School in the Washington Heights section of Manhattan. Mostly poor blacks and Dominicans lived in the neighborhood, and the groups often didn't get along well. I never really gave my all in school, because I was more fascinated with life beyond the school walls.

Living in Harlem during the eighties didn't make going to school any easier. The neighborhood was energetic, fast-paced, and full of diversions. You would always see older cats hanging out and hustling on the corner. They gathered on the corners, hustled, and shot dice for money all night long. Cats would be outside playing ceelo and craps, gambling all night until police rolled up to the scene and made them leave.

If there was no block party or jam on your block, you

could easily find one if you walked long enough. Neighborhood parks like the Battlegrounds and Rucker's sponsored popular basketball tournaments complete with some of the hottest music and the finest girls in the 'hood.

The world-famous Apollo Theater on 125th Street hosted its legendary Amateur Night on Wednesdays, where you got to see and hear the best and worst entertainment of the day for a reasonable price. If the act was hot, the audience showed love. Hustlers would sit in the balcony section and throw wads of money on stage for kid acts or fine female dance groups. Bad acts sometimes got objects thrown at them along with profanity and screams to "get the fuck outta here!"

Also on 125th Street were several street vendors who sold everything from books to clothes, African jewelry, paintings, and fragrances. It was the black version of Delancey Street, where a customer could haggle prices with a vendor and walk away with good products at a discount.

These days, you can play video games on the Internet or on a console at home. But I came up before the Nintendo, PlayStation, and Xbox generations. If you didn't have an Atari console at home, you gathered some quarters and went to the local game room to play video games like Space Invaders, Pac-Man, Asteroids, or Centipede. Jumbo pizza slices cost under a dollar, and many pizza shops had video games, so kids would stay in game rooms all day. That is, until game room owners banned kids from playing games until after three p.m.

Harlem has always been known for its restaurants and

hole-in-the-wall food spots. Mr. Stokes and his two sons owned a grocery store. I remember the 721 restaurant—Frank's Italian spot—that had some good chicken and spaghetti. My mom used to send me there all the time to pick up an order. Mr. Steve owned the Texas Star Diner restaurant. That spot had some of the best breakfast in Harlem. One of my favorite dishes was beef sausage and scrambled eggs with cheese and a half and half (ice tea mixed with lemonade).

Harlem also had some of the best fish and chip spots. One of the most famous was a little hole-in-the-wall joint called Famous Fish, located right on 145th Street and St. Nick. The spot was so small that only about five people could fit in there at one time. People came from all over New York City and stood in line during the summer just to get some of that mouthwatering fish! In fact, Famous Fish is still going strong today.

Besides all of these distractions, school didn't hold my attention because I just couldn't see how school would help my situation. I observed that an education did not always guarantee employment, at least not good employment. I knew very few people who'd graduated from college, and most of my friends who graduated high school weren't doing much better than the high school dropouts. Why waste time pursuing an education that didn't pay off?

By ninth grade, during the winter of 1980, I made the decision to drop out of high school. I remember the day I left school for good. It was snowing outside, and I felt sick. I left during sixth period, at about 1:30 p.m. I exited through the gate and saw tons of Dominican cats standing across the street. These cats were wild, and they always gave black students a hard time. The gate locked behind me, so I couldn't reenter the school.

I decided to walk past the cats. First one snowball hit, then another, then more flew by me. I yelled "Fuck you, motherfuckers!" and they all ran after me. I remember thinking that I just didn't want to go back to school anymore. It seemed like I had few reasons to stay and a million reasons to leave.

Now I regret my indifferent attitude toward education; if I could go back in time I would do things differently. Investing in your education is investing in yourself, and giving yourself more options in life. I urge students to make the most of their time in school.

I've lived in other parts of New York City throughout my life, but Harlem, especially Sugar Hill, will always be my home.

4
Temptations

It's important to remember that drug dealers—or any members of the criminal underworld—*are not criminals from birth*. They are born pure and innocent children, like the rest of us. Desperate circumstances can make it easy for some people to begin lives of crime.

My introduction to the hustling game happened in 1983. I worked at Mr. Jimmy's dry cleaners at the time. Every Saturday morning I opened the shop at seven a.m. All the old-timers, big shots, and numbers bankers would hang out there on Saturdays, talking shit and placing big bets.

The numbers was a game of chance that began in Harlem during the 1920s. People would go to a numbers spot in the 'hood and wager money that a particular three-digit number would hit. If the number hit, you won. The winning number was randomly drawn from the attendance at horse races. A certain race was chosen, and then later that day, the newspaper recorded the number of people that attended the race. The last three numbers became the winning number.

A runner would go throughout the neighborhood collecting money and recording people's bets on slips of paper. As with any game of chance, the odds were always against the bettors. The numbers banker received money whether people hit or not, so bankers tended to net huge sums of money.

The numbers bankers took a liking to me. I was a nice kid, I didn't talk much, and I was a good listener. "You have two ears and one mouth—that means you should do more listening and less talking." "Always respect your elders, and mind your business at all times." Mr. Jimmy dropped those bits of advice on me.

Most of these cats were rich bar owners who ran local after-hours joints. As such, they were aware of all the latest news and events going on in the 'hood. Listening to those guys talk helped me understand what to do and not to do in the hustling game.

One of the richest of them all was a cat named June. I loved his style. He would bet big, talk the least shit, and his number seemed to always play: 418. He was lucky. More important to me, he seemed to be in control of his own world. When everybody dressed up and wore fine jewelry, Mr. June was humble and silent. He got love without being flashy. But when it was time for June to throw it on, he wore tailor-made suits and alligator shoes. Everybody looked up to Mr. June.

Temptations

Another older brother who made an impact on me was Mr. Wilson. He owned the famous Wilson's Bakery on 158th Street and Amsterdam Avenue. He was also best friends with Mr. Jimmy. Whenever those two got together, you knew sparks were going to fly. Mr. Wilson cracked jokes on Mr. Jimmy all the time. He said things like, "Close this piece of shit cleaner's down. I'll pay you what you make each week, just for hanging out with me." His bakery made a killing, and he never wanted Mr. Jimmy to forget it.

Meanwhile, another generation began running things on the streets. Their business wasn't numbers, though. It was a lot harder: narcotics like heroin and cocaine. I never met these cats but I heard a lot about them, and saw them drive by in nice whips (expensive cars).

Mr. Wilson always complained about the young hustlers selling drugs right around the corner from his bakery. He was totally against drug selling. Whenever he complained about the young hustlers, Mr. Jimmy would tell him to mind his business.

One day Mr. Wilson boldly stepped to the brothers and asked them to move their drug operation away from his bakery. The hustlers looked at Mr. Wilson like he was crazy. To them, he was a problem. Mr. Wilson asked them a few more times to move their operation, and the young cats still ignored him. Finally, Mr. Wilson had enough and decided to call the police.

Officers rolled on the scene one day, and arrested one of the cats. The young hustlers finally moved their operation to avoid heat from the police. Within a couple of months, the young cats retaliated. Mr. Wilson was shot to death while heading home one evening, gunned down in cold blood.

Mr. Jimmy was devastated by the news of his friend's death. He'd constantly told Mr. Wilson to mind his own business and leave it alone. But Mr. Wilson didn't listen, and it cost him his life.

People like Mr. Jimmy and Mr. Wilson—cats in their fifties—taught me a great deal about the game. But the person who inspired me most was a particular young hustler. One bright, sunny day I was running down St. Nick dribbling a basketball. As I passed a garage on 145th Street, a car pulled out real fast and knocked me to the ground. I looked up to the nose of a brand-new BMW 735. The driver got out and started talking:

"Yo, shorty, are you alright?"

I got up and looked in awe at this spacecraft. It was black with lavender lamb seats that sported black bat emblems.

"Shorty, are you alright?"

I had to snap out of it.

"Yeah, I'm alright."

"Yo, you gotta watch where you going, son."

He pulled out a wad of money and peeled off a one-hundred-dollar bill.

"Here, shorty. Put this in your pocket. Keep your head up."

He jumped back into his UFO playing William DeVaughan's song "Be thankful for what you got."

Temptation: I wanted to be just like this cat. I wanted to be able to pull out a knot of money, jump back into my spaceship, and fly away like it was nothing. I guess that's the day I was bitten by the bat. That experience planted the seed of hustling in my mind. A couple of days later, I ran into my man Rich Porter. I knew Rich because we lived on the same block, and we'd attended elementary school together. I spoke to him about the situation. Rich knew all about the fast life. He had his ear to the streets, so he knew who I was talking about.

"Oh, that's Bat," Rich said. "He's down with Jerome. His whip is crazy too. He drives a white BMW 635 with the white steering wheel. His crew picked up where Nicky Barnes and Guy Fisher left off. Their clique is real strong."

This shit sounded like a movie and I wanted to be in it. I felt that this was my time. Every generation brings forth a new breed and our generation was next in line. Look at it this way: The cats two generations before us listened to eight-track tapes. The cats after them listened to cassette tapes. In my era, compact discs replaced cassettes. Now people don't even have to purchase tapes, compact discs, or albums. Today, people download music on iPods or listen to satellite radio. In other words, technology has transformed the way we do things.

Back in the mid-eighties, young cats wanted to be like, dress like, and talk like the older cats in the streets. When you met someone, the first thing you did was look them up and down. You looked at his shoes first. The shoe game had to be tight. To be considered cool, you had to rock name-brand sneakers like Pro Keds, Converse, shell-toe Adidas, or Nikes. For shoes, you wore Playboys or British

Walkers to go with your AJ's slacks overlaps. Then you could top it off with a Corderfields corduroy coat with the fox collar.

Your kicks had to be fresh! Rich Porter always kept a new pair of kicks on his feet. His favorites were the white-on-white Reebok Classics; they went with any of his many outfits, and believe me, he had many. No outfit was complete without a splash of champagne, or cologne. To stay fresh, people flooded stores like Vets or Guys and Gals on 125th Street, Apple Town on 145th Street and Seventh Avenue, and K.P. Kong's on 145th and Broadway. Sometimes we would skate over to the Bronx to get clothes at Jew Man's, at half price.

Once you got your wardrobe tight, you needed something to get around in. You might start with a simple ten-speed bike. The most popular at the time was the Peugeot ten-speed. If you couldn't afford that, you bought the Apollo five-speed. My man Toot actually lost his left nut riding that bike. The next popular form of transportation was mopeds, which were motor scooters.

The Champ was the most popular moped out in the eighties. Fast Kid was the first one I saw with one of those joints; it was yellow and white. I had to have one of those too. I got lucky one day, when I played a number for one dollar and hit for six hundred dollars. It was just enough for me to get a yellow-and-white Champ!

Dirt bikes like the YZ became the new thing after motor scooters. Rich and L.A. put on shows with their dirt bikes, doing wheelies, doughnuts, and burnouts, up and down Seventh and Lenox Avenues. Police chased them as people on the sidewalks cheered them on. They always managed to get away.

L.A. was popular in Harlem. For one thing, he was the youngest brother around the way with his own car. He was only about fifteen years old when he first started getting big money in Harlem. On top of that, he was slick-talking, played basketball well, and the girls thought he was cute. He was outspoken and had a magnetic personality. When he spoke or did anything, you wanted to be around to say you were there. He and Rich were young cats, both getting crazy money from dealing heroin in the 'hood. They were also the first young cats I saw making big paper and flossing cars and jewelry.

I first met L.A. in 1982 through my man Rich. He bet L.A. one hundred dollars that I could beat him in a one-on-one game of basketball. I was pretty good in ball back then. We went over to meet L.A. at Drew Hamilton projects on 144th Street and Eighth Avenue. A lot of people showed up to see the one-on-one game. L.A. wound up winning, and Rich lost his money, but I got to meet the legendary L.A. Both he and Rich would go on to set Harlem on fire with the flashy cars they brought on the block.

L.A. busted out with the Saab 900 Turbo. It was black-on-black with white piping and a chrome exhaust pipe. Within a month's time, Rich busted out with the black-on-black BMW 528. It had the black-and-white lamb seats. Another hustler from uptown had the burgundy BMW 535. His man came through with the black Volvo wagon and another had the Jeep Wagoneer.

Unbelievable! These cats were just out of junior high

school. The girls in our 'hood went crazy for them. On the street level, they were more popular than the Jacksons. I was just working at the cleaners, but I was in love with the game. The temptation was growing.

I was riding with Rich and L.A. in the BMW 528 one day. It felt like we were floating around Harlem, the mecca of all 'hoods. Little George with the big Afro had just blessed the BMW with one of his famous car washes, so the car was laced . . . . clean as a motherfucker!

We stopped at the light, and this young girl pulled up on our left. She was driving a brand-new candy-apple-red Porsche 911 Carrera. She must have just cleaned her car too, because it still had Armor All leaking from the tires. She looked in our car, gave us a sexy wink, and pulled off doing like one hundred miles an hour, playing "I Want You" by Marvin Gaye. L.A. started talking about her soon as she pulled off.

"Yo, Dick, I told you she liked me. I gotta have her."

"Yo, Mels got her man wide open," replied Rich. "He's in love. He got her driving a 911 Carrera."

Shaking his head, L.A. said, "All I know is that Melody is a bad young chick. I'm gonna get that!"

L.A. wasn't lying about the girl's looks. Melody was a pretty, sexy, soft-talking, smooth, butterscotch, vanilla wafer, caramel baby doll with the perfectly round and plump JLo or Beyoncé ass. The way I saw it, she was the Cleopatra of our 'hood.

"Mel's got these older bitches out here fucked up," commented Rich. "Fourteen years old and handling a Porsche like that."

I was in the backseat, fucked up myself. The girl was only fourteen and driving a Porsche? I couldn't even afford a bike. "This shit is crazy," I thought. *Temptation.*

Within a few months, L.A.'s dream came true. Melody's man was killed on the dance floor at his own birthday party. Of course Melody was hurt and things went a little sour for her. She hooked up with L.A., they fell in love, and had a healthy baby boy. We called him "Baby L." Mels was used to the finer things in life, and L.A. was no slouch. He laced her with a new Renault Fuego. It wasn't a Porsche, but it was hot at the time.

Like most fine girls, Melody had some fine-ass friends too: Cupcake, Lori Love, Debbie Parker, Pumpkin, and her two sisters Debbie and Crystal. They were known as the Bowery Girls. They hung out right across the street from the Big Track 356, old man Marshall's gambling spot. A lot of gangsters and big shots won and lost hundreds of thousands of dollars in there every other night.

Moments after Melody pulled off, we parked on 125th Street and Eighth Avenue. We went into a store called A.J. Lesters, where all the hustlers shopped for the latest gear.

Rich and L.A. must have spent about $2,500 apiece preparing to go to the Jacksons concert at Madison Square Garden that night. I thought to myself, "What the hell is going on here? I'm working hard in the local cleaners, running the place, pressing, cleaning, and tailoring. I run the business seven days a week for only seventy-five dollars." Rich and L.A. might tip a barber or waiter more than that!

That night I tossed and turned and never managed to

get any sleep. I kept replaying the scenes from earlier that day: Melody driving around in that hot car, and my boys pulling out knots of money to buy hot clothes. I had seen enough. I wanted in.

While Rich and L.A. moved heroin, I tried bootlegging liquor on Sundays. That hustle didn't pay off. A one-day flip wasn't good enough. Turning $75 into $150 every weekend wasn't that big a payoff for the effort involved.

Then the great temptation came that changed my life. The movie *Scarface* came out in 1983. It wasn't just a movie. It was a big, entertaining commercial promoting the sale and use of cocaine!

The film's main character, Tony Montana, put the battery in me. I was charged after viewing that piece, and Harlem fell right into the trap. That movie put cocaine on the map. Many cats from the 'hood wanted to go from rags to riches like Tony did. It seemed like cocaine was the ticket out of poverty.

By working in the cleaners and making deliveries, I was apparently in the right place at the right time. I met this Colombian cocaine dealer named Lulu. Some time around 1983, Lulu gave me my first package and introduced me to the fast life.

Lulu was a cool, smooth dude. He had jet-black, curly hair that he wore in a ponytail. He didn't speak English that well, but I knew where he was coming from when he spoke. A lot of cats from the 'hood knew Lulu from the poolroom he owned on 157th Street between Broadway and Amsterdam. He and I had a different relationship: We did business from his house.

Temptations

He wasted no time in schooling me: "For you, Azito, lesson number one. Don't ever get high off of your product, it will make you loco. Number two, don't ever tell anyone about me. Number three, stay low, and always follow instructions. Trust me, and money will never be a problem for you."

"Money will never be a problem." Those were the words any young kid in the ghetto wanted to hear at that time. The influences of *Scarface* and that crazy ride with Rich and L.A. had me thinking. I began to weigh my circumstances. I thought about my poor dear mother and hardworking father, struggling to support my five sisters and two brothers. I thought about the embarrassment we felt when we had to hide my father from the welfare workers who constantly threatened to cut off the little bit of money we received each month.

What would you have done? Situations like mine might tempt many people to break the law. I swear I didn't choose the game, the game chose me. Lulu gave me my first package, and I took it to the streets.

After I got the work from Lulu, I needed someone to check it out and make sure it wasn't bullshit. I have to share this funny-ass story about this cat named Slim the Desert Fox. I loved this cat. Slim was the neighborhood numbers runner. In fact, he was the one I won the $600 with earlier. I could talk to him because he was down to earth. When Slim made his rounds, he would stick his head in the cleaners and call out the number that played.

Slim was a country boy originally from Mississippi. He stood about six foot five, and was very skinny. Slim drove a long Fleetwood Cadillac. It was probably the only car he could fit in. One thing I remember about Slim was that he said the word "nigga" about one thousand times a minute in conversation, and he was always in trouble for fucking somebody's woman.

One day Slim stuck his head in the store to call out the number. I anxiously called him to the back of the store. Slim was his usual funny and energetic self.

"What do you want with me, little nigga? You wanna place a bet or something? Put your money where your mouth is, little nigga. I'm on the move; time is money, and money is time." I pulled out some cocaine wrapped in aluminum foil and showed Slim.

"What the fuck is this, little nigga?" He stuck his finger in and tasted it. His eyes opened wide.

"Where the fuck did you get this blow from, little nigga?"

Acting like a big shot I said, "Don't worry, there's much more where that came from. I need you to check it out for me."

Slim recognized me stunting and replied, "Aw, little nigga, you ain't saying nothing slick. I'm the Desert Fox. I'll buy this little bit of shit from you right now" as he slid me a fifty-dollar bill. He took the coke and said, "I'll be back with your reading, little nigga."

"Yo, Slim, where you going?" I asked. "I need you to tell me if it's good or not."

"Be quiet, little nigga. Let me go test it out. I'll be back soon. Hold your head. Sit tight, little nigga."

Slim left and returned the next day. The Fox's whole

head was bandaged up, and he had a bloody cotton ball in his nose. He grabbed me and pulled me to the back of the cleaners.

"Little nigga, what the fuck was that shit you gave me?"

I put my hands up in defense and replied, "That was supposed to be coke."

"Put your hands down, little nigga. I'm not gonna hurt you. Where did you get it from?"

I wanted to respect and protect what Lulu told me, so I said, "That's not important, Slim."

"What you mean, that's not important! Look at my nose, little nigga!"

I put my hands back up.

"I said, keep your hands down, little nigga. I'm not gonna hurt you."

Slim pulled out about $500 and said, "Get me some more of that shit right now. That's the best shit I ever had! You keep it like that, and you'll make millions. I thought you had some bullshit, but you got the best fish scale from Peru! Take this five hundred, and bring me some back immediately!"

"But what about your nose, Slim?" I asked.

"Don't worry about that, *big* nigga. I'll be fine. This time I'll be careful."

Wow! I went from "little nigga" to "big nigga." I got my reading, and it was time to open up shop. I couldn't stop customers from coming to the cleaners and knocking on the window. They were walking back and forth, and waiting for me out front. It was getting crazy. I knew eventually that my job would be in jeopardy, so I would tell the customers to stop coming by during my work hours. But the narcotics that Lulu gave me were so good and so cheap, the fiends paid no attention to me.

Mr. Jimmy saw all the traffic in front of his store, and he wasn't a fool. Things were getting too crazy. For instance, one day a fiend came in the cleaners and asked Mr. Jimmy if I could come outside to speak to him for a minute. When I returned, Mr. Jimmy flipped on me.

"Azie . . . what the fuck are you doing? Why all these bum motherfuckas coming around looking for you? I hope you're not selling no drugs out of my store."

"Naw, naw, Mr. Jimmy . . . what you talking about? I don't sell no drugs," I responded.

"Don't make me have to call your mother. All of a sudden, these motherfuckas start knocking on my windows asking for you. What else could you be doing with them? You don't use drugs, do you?"

"No, Mr. Jimmy . . ."

"And you better not have no fuckin' drugs stashed in this motherfucka. 'Cause if the police come up in here and find *anything*, you better own up to it! I'm not doing no time for no fuckin' body . . . you hear me?"

"Yeah, Mr. Jimmy."

I respected Mr. Jimmy a lot, and I really needed that job for cover. But on another note, I was in "bed" with Lulu. Seventy-five dollars a week compared to seventy-five dollars every five minutes was a big difference!

Like I said, Mr. Jimmy was no fool; he knew what time it was and he knew the game was calling me and pulling me in. I used to stash my drugs in the pocket of an old trench coat toward the back of the cleaners. I reached in the coat pocket one day, and my stash was gone . . . the pocket was empty! I turned around and there was Mr. Jimmy holding my stash.

"You looking for this?"

I dropped my head in shame. "Now he's gonna call my mother," I thought. He started to scold me.

"Do you know what you're getting yourself into? Don't you know this shit can cost you your life? You can get murdered if you don't pay up on time. You can get life in prison. Oh, I know what it is. You wanna be like the Porter kid from Amsterdam Avenue, the one that comes in here with all those fancy clothes. I know what he does. You think I'm blind to the streets? That I don't know what the fuck is going on? Take your shit and get the fuck out. You're done here! Matter of fact, I'm gonna call your mother and let her know, 'cause I don't need this shit on my conscience."

At that point, I gave Mr. Jimmy a vicious look that said: *You better not tell my mother.* I snatched my stuff, told him to mind his fucking business, and left the cleaners. I'd just gotten into the drug game and already I flipped on a brother that had been good to me. Before I got the drugs, I wouldn't have dreamed about talking to Mr. Jimmy like I did that day.

To my knowledge, Mr. Jimmy never did tell my mother about me hustling. I would still see him around the way and always speak. I knew Mr. Jimmy remembered how his best friend was killed for trying to scold a young hustler. I wondered if he thought I would do to him what the young dealer had done to Mr. Wilson.

The 5 Game

Why do so many youth risk their lives and freedom to sell drugs? The explanation is simple. We live in a materialistic society where you must make money to live nicely. If you don't have a strong education or marketable job skills to get paid, it's likely that you will turn to crime.

I saw older cats driving expensive cars, wearing flashy clothes, and hanging out with the finest women I'd ever seen. Harlem was literally flooded with drugs, especially heroin, cocaine, and weed. I saw two options staring at me: use drugs and get fucked up by circumstances, or sell drugs and use circumstances to survive.

You might have heard these sayings before: "You have to crawl before you walk." "You have to be an Indian before you can be a chief." Some say you have to be scouted before you make it to the big leagues. That's how the game goes.

Game Over

Competition is a major part of any game, and when it comes to the drug game, competition has no end. Jealousy, envy, hate, greed, and the love of money often make the outcome of the game ugly.

I was hustling hard. I was on my grind and it seemed like I blew up overnight. The moon was full, and my fangs had fully grown. I had my cape, and all I needed was my electrum, my ride, my UFO. Within a month's time, I bought a rust-colored Toyota Corolla. Dudes laughed at my joint, but inside I thought, "That's okay, I'm gonna stay low like Lulu told me."

By the time a month passed, I couldn't take the jokes anymore. I bought a baby Benz 190, gold-on-gold with black-and-gold lamb seats. "Paid in full. Laugh now niggas," I thought. I came through creeping, with my sound system bumping "Nobody Can Be You" by Steve Arrington. I gave the Toyota to my lady, Patricia Porter.

Pat was Rich's little sister. I knew her damn near all my life, but we didn't start dating until about 1980. Pat came to the cleaners all the time with her brother's clothes. When I had to deliver clothes to Rich, me and Pat would sit in her house and talk. We became friends over the years, and Pat would start coming to the cleaners just to see me. By the time I gave the Toyota to Pat in 1984, she had just given birth to my firstborn, my baby girl Lorrell Faison.

Before long, Rich and L.A. were riding in my car! They couldn't understand it. They wanted to know what I did to get paid so fast. I told them how I operated, and got them a brick—a kilo—of cocaine. They set up shop on

144th Street and Seventh Avenue. Soon, money came in by the duffel bags, just like it did for Tony Montana in *Scarface*. Looking back, I can say that making all that money made us blind to destroying our own. But at the time, we wanted to live large.

And we did live large. Rich hopped in a new Jeep Wagoneer. L.A. jumped in a black Jeep Laredo, came through with the top off, windshield dropped down, with no doors. L.A. and Rich proudly rode around Harlem, bumping the song "Look at California," by Maze featuring Frankie Beverly.

One day Rich, L.A., and their man Cee-Moe were driving a brand-new, rimmed-out, black-on-black BMW with black rims. It was a beautiful foreign car that was bound to attract the attention of cops. Sure enough, the cops pulled them over. The officers pulled them out the car and began to search them. Me and other young cats watched from across the street, hoping they didn't get locked up.

After questioning them about wearing bulletproof vests, the police let them go! Rich calmly jumped back into his ride like nothing happened. He pulled off blowing his horn as he winked his eye at me. To young cats in the 'hood, that was some gangster shit! Minutes later, Sean Mo blew past in the brown 300 ZX T-top. Those were the days when every kid in our 'hood wanted to be like them. If you didn't, you were considered a sucka. That was the game.

Rich and L.A. were the talk of the town. The word "popular" could not begin to describe their status. The spell they cast on everyone was truly amazing.

Drama! Then that night comes you get that sad phone call.

"Hello, who this?"

"It's me, A, Rich."

I heard the sadness in his voice. I asked, "What happened?"

"L.A. got shot," Rich replied.

I was shocked. "L.A. got shot?"

"Yeah, he was at the Rooftop."

The Rooftop was a popular roller-skating rink and club located on 155th Street and Eighth Avenue. Everybody in the hood went to the Rooftop. L.A., who was a real smooth skater, often spent time there. Rich warned L.A. to stay out of that joint, because he felt jealousy in the air.

I rushed over to Harlem Hospital, and found tons of people already there with their fingers crossed for L.A., hoping that he would live. Soon after I arrived, someone reported the news that L.A. didn't make it. "No, not L.A.," I thought. It was a sad night for Harlem. A crowd of people stayed in front of the hospital all night, crying and hoping it didn't really happen. It was news that the 'hood found hard to swallow.

I never really got the chance to hang out much with L.A. before he was killed. He treated me with respect, and news of his death hit me hard. Everybody in the 'hood was a fan of L.A.'s. whether we knew him personally or not. To us, he was a young brother who had money and lived life to the fullest.

His funeral was held at the famous funeral home, Bentas, on the corner of 141st Street and St. Nicholas Avenue.

The Game

It seemed like all of Harlem paid their respects, young and old, in tears. So many people loved Donald "L.A." Johnson. L.A.'s death devastated his family. His mother, Ms. Marbell, was shattered, as L.A. was her heart.

L.A. had a good friend named Bunky who was serving time for a shootout with the police. I heard he started to lose his mind in the penitentiary behind the news of L.A.'s death.

Melody was terrified. L.A. had been murdered just like her previous boyfriend, and she had seen enough. She took their son, Donald Johnson, Jr., and moved out of New York state.

I never did know the exact story behind L.A.'s death, but I had suspicions. I thought back to a prior incident in front of this Italian restaurant named 721. Rich, L.A., and Cee-Moe walked toward me. I was about to greet them, when Rich put his finger to his lips as a signal for me to be quiet. I knew something was about to go down, so I walked across the street.

A dude exited the restaurant, and I saw Rich and his boys approach the guy. I was too far away to hear the conversation, but the body language told me they were beefing with the cat. The next thing I knew, Rich and L.A. began to empty their guns out on the guy, and then they took off down the block. From what I heard, it sounded like they shot him about twenty-four times. The guy struggled to get up, then started returning the fire. He threw his gun in the street under a car and jumped in a cab.

Talk on the streets revealed that the dude's name was Ras Clad, and L.A. suspected he was involved in the robbery of his mother's house a month earlier. The guy wore a bullet-proof vest that day, and he survived the shooting. Everybody thought this dude Ras Clad had L.A. killed in retaliation.

Ras Clad eventually lost his life in the streets years later. The game was getting ugly, because of greed and violence. L.A., like so many other youth, had become another statistic of the streets.

After L.A.'s death, things got real hot. DTs—detectives—were all over the place. Within a couple of months things began to quiet down. Business was back to normal. I was moving, making it happen. Rich, on the other hand, had to keep a low profile. Some of L.A.'s homies thought that Rich had something to do with L.A.'s murder; their theory was that Rich killed L.A. to keep all their drug profits to himself. I know in my heart that wasn't the case, because Rich saw L.A. as his brother.

A few months later, two stick-up kids tried to rob Rich's girlfriend's house on 140th Street. One of the stick-up kids was killed in the process. The word on the street was that one of them accidentally shot the other and ran. Things got crazy for Rich, and he armed up to protect himself. Sometimes he wore a bulletproof vest, and he kept nine-millimeter handguns in various stash spots and cars. Rich warned me to be careful, to stay low, and to stay "sucker free," his way of warning me to avoid jealous cats.

One day in 1985 two cats ran up and fired shots at Rich while he sat in his Jeep in a car wash. Rich pulled out his nine-millimeter and started firing back, chasing them as they ran for cover. Police rushed the scene and Rich was arrested.

The Game

Rich got a year for the gun charge and did his whole bid on Riker's Island. Pat was hurt and really nervous for her brother. She didn't know what was going on. All she knew was that she didn't want her brother dead. Pat and Rich's girl Yolanda visited him regularly; they never missed a visit.

But, the show had to continue. So I started spreading out, doing business with new cats who were boys of Rich (with his permission, of course). Fast Kid DB, a young fly kid, grew up with Rich and they were very close. There were several other Harlem cats I dealt with. I gave these cats my recipe and formula for making plenty of dough.

Nick and Blue's crew—Fats (also known as "Tray Bag,"), Yummy, black Otis, and Chin—had a vicious shootout; fortunately no one was killed. This made the block wide open for me to do my thing. After a while, things got a little hot around there, and I had to leave. I resisted leaving because Sugar Hill was my stomping grounds, my 'hood.

Tons of money always flowed through my neighborhood. Why? Our operation was located right by some of Harlem's hottest nightspots. You had the Blue Book and the Mark V bar, Patsy Bar was down the block, Lundy's and the pub the Jazz Spot were right around the way too.

In that same area, you had this after-hours spot called the Zodiac, and the S&S club. Heavy gambling took place in these joints every other night. Right downstairs from the S&S club on 145th Street and Eighth Avenue was the world-famous Willie's Burger, where all the pretty, sexy chicks would sport their fancy hairdos and dress up in expensive furs and minks. They were there to watch the young hustlers showcase their jewelry and their exotic cars.

People from all over would show up: the Bronx, Brooklyn, Queens, you name it. Mount Vernon, Yonkers ("Y.O."), and Connecticut represented as well. Right around the corner was the Ponderosa and another spot called Triggers where people partied all night long.

While cats partied all night, I was right across the street putting in work. It was funny to see dudes break day in those nightspots, then come out when the sun was up. When that bright sunlight hit them, it was like they had seen God, and they'd run back inside. There's no doubt about it . . . in the 1980s, Harlem was the jump off.

I opened up a game room called The Jukebox on 145th Street between Seventh and Eighth Avenues. My brother Kev, my man Stan, Lou, and a bunch of other cats had the joint jumping. Chico, aka "Cheek La Freak" and my man Dog Food provided security and my sister Robin managed the candy section of the business. We had a jukebox that played actual music videos, a variety of arcade games, and snacks. It was off the hook.

We blasted the hottest rap songs out: "Larry's Dance Theme" by Grandmaster Flash and the Furious Five, "King of Rock" by Run DMC, and "Freaks Come Out at Night" by Whodini, just to name a few. My spot became a favorite hangout in the 'hood, and my whole crew was getting paid.

When I first started hustling, a cousin of mine came to me one time and said, "Yo, Zee, I got some work I want you to move for me. Come in the hallway for a minute."

The Game

So we went in the hallway. He was looking around like we were going to make a major deal or something. He whipped out some coke in a glassine bag and handed it to me asking, "How long will it take you to move this?"

I poured it in my hand and asked how much he wanted for it. He looked around like he was about to reveal classified information before giving me the answer. "Give me fifty dollars for this. How much time do you need to move it?" I looked at the coke in my hand and looked back at him. I blew the coke off my palm and watched as the powder drifted in the air. My bold action shocked him.

"What the fuck are you doing, man?"

"I just moved the coke. Was that quick enough?" Before he could respond, I tossed him the fifty dollars he wanted. "Oh yeah," he replied. "That was fast. I'll see you tomorrow." He came back the next day and I gave him a job.

Once you get money and you earn power and respect, everyone wants to join the team. Sometime in 1985, my man Lou told me that a cat named Alpo wanted to meet me. He introduced himself to Lou one night at the Rooftop. I knew Alpo was cool with my man Rich, so I agreed to meet with him in my game room.

Alpo was from the east side, or Spanish Harlem. He was a half black, half Puerto Rican, pretty-boy thug, about three years younger than me. He told me a lot about his past and said he was ready to do his own thing. He told me he had a good crack clientele. Rich used to give him work before getting locked up; 'Po needed a new connection now.

One thing led to another—I spoke to Rich, and he gave

me the green light to work with 'Po. When we met again, I gave Alpo some work and shared my recipe for making money. He never looked back. Once he made up his mind to do something, 'Po made it happen. He was assertive like that.

What I respected about Alpo was that he didn't waste time with middlemen. He sought out bosses because he knew they had the power to get the job done. For example, one time in '85, 'Po pulled up in a U-Haul truck.

"Yo, big A, get in. Get in and ride with me, man."

"Where you going with this big-ass truck, man? What you got in there, some kilos or a whole lot of money?"

'Po laughed as I got in and we made our way to Crazy Eddie's, an electronics shop on Fordham Road in the Bronx. Alpo asked for the store manager.

"Are you the boss? You make decisions around here?"

"Yes, why?" asked the manager.

"I'm looking for the best deal, that's why!"

With that, Alpo told him he wanted to buy two of the biggest televisions they had in stock. The manager took us to a storage room and showed us two sixty-inch televisions. They cost about $5,000 each.

"Look, how much you gonna charge me for both?"

The manager replied that he could knock off the taxes. Alpo peeled off $10,000 from his pocket and handed it to the manager. The manager went to do the paperwork. Minutes later, two police officers came in and asked to search us. They found two vials of crack on Alpo and arrested him. I stayed behind to get the televisions and load them into the truck.

The Game

When Alpo got out, he came to me saying, "Yo, A, the cops that locked me up told me that the store manager called them after I paid for those TV sets. I wanna go get at that nigga. All I did was try to bring the dude some business."

I knew 'Po wasn't bullshittin' and he had a gun in his waist. I calmed him down, and we moved on. No nonsense, no time to waste, no fucking with middlemen . . . that was the type of cat 'Po was.

I recall riding up 128th near Eighth Avenue one summer day. An older brother drove past us in a Corvette Sting Ray. It was one of the prettiest cars I'd ever seen. 'Po honked for the dude to pull over and he did. I'm sure he had mutual admiration for the car we drove. The guy pulled over and Alpo stepped to him. Within ten minutes, 'Po made him a deal he couldn't refuse—he wanted the guy's car so bad that he offered to pay him a huge lump sum right on the spot. The guy agreed, so Alpo went to the trunk, pulled out a bag of money, and handed it to the guy. The guy jumped in a cab, smiling from ear to ear. 'Po pulled off in the Corvette, and I trailed him in the BMW.

Partly from jealousy, cats on the street told me I created a monster. They wasted no time reminding me of Alpo's humble beginnings or his reputation as a stickup kid. "A, that nigga was just riding around in fucked-up hot rods, now that he's fucking with you, he getting hot joints," they'd say. Hot rods were cheap little cars assembled from a variety of different parts. They usually sported fat tires and super loud sound systems.

I wasn't the type that liked to gossip; I was chasing

paper. I never took the bad words about Alpo seriously. I never liked when a cat would shit on the next man to gain respect. Was I supposed to stop working with Alpo because of street rumors from jealous cats? I didn't get down like that. I would tell the gossiping cats to leave the clown shit back home in their dresser or closet. "Don't bring that bullshit around me," I would tell them. If they needed help or wanted to work with me, all they had to do was be a man and ask. If they talked behind cats' backs, how could I trust them anyway?

I didn't care about Alpo's background, and I didn't see him as a threat. He never did anything to violate me. He always paid me on time, and he played fair. I believe he never stepped to me wrong, because I was the one who set him up in the game. I gave him the opportunity to be a boss. Prior to dealing with me, he always worked under someone else. The Alpo I knew loved me and Rich.

Alpo and I became tight. I honestly felt I could trust him with my life. He knew where I lived. As a matter of fact, he had the keys to one of my apartments in Lenox Terrace, where I kept plenty of money, and he didn't steal a penny. He was loyal to me. We had an overstanding.

I trusted the brother enough to hook him up with shit. One summer day, Alpo came with me to pick up a new Volvo station wagon. A new sports car called the Impulse was on display. It looked real slick. Alpo couldn't take his eyes off the car.

"This shit is hot! It's crazy!"

After paying for the wagon, I asked 'Po if he liked the car.

The Game

"Hell, yeah! That shit is crazy, A," he replied.

I called the dealer over and asked about the price. The dealer said it was about $18,000 and $21,000 with taxes.

"Yo, Alpo, you want it?"

"Yeah. What you think?" Alpo replied.

I bought it for him right on the spot. The black Impulse was the talk of the town.

Alpo also looked out for me. I remember one time he drove up smiling, saying he had something for me. He knew that counting money was a huge, time-consuming job, so he bought me a money-counting machine. It could hold about 150 bills at once, and could count up to 1,000 bills a minute.

Alpo wasn't the only one for whom I bought a car. I bought my man Lou a Fiat and a Cadillac Seville. Stan got an Audi 4000. I put this chick named Leslie in a Mazda 626. Patricia got a Jetta, an Acura, and a blue Sterling. I bought my mom two Volvo station wagons. My sister Robin got a custom-made drop-top Toyota Celica.

Business was good and I liked to share the wealth. It meant nothing to me because I knew I couldn't take the money with me after death. Besides, knowing I'd done something to make a person happy was one of the best feelings in the world.

We were onstage and we had to perform. I copped the cherry-red Saab drop-top 900 turbo, the first one in the United States. The first day I bought it I came through playing that Cameo hit "Candy" and the chicks went crazy. When we drove those cars, all you saw were streaks of colors skating up and down Lenox Avenue.

Game Over

We were way ahead of our time, and the 'hood showed us mad love and respect. Like 'Po, I was in love with cars. It was like a drug and I was addicted.

One night while heading up the Major Deegan Expressway with this chick named Pinky, I did 190 miles an hour in a Hammer AMG Benz. The shit felt like it was about to take flight! I blew past the police so fast that they didn't even attempt to chase me. That was a mean machine!

At the Apollo Theater, my car made plenty of heads turn. My little man Whip jumped out of the joint stunting. "Yeah, yeah, yeah, you know what it is, get back, get back. We're not signing any autographs tonight."

I felt the love, and I felt the hate.

The average person gets frustrated when they purchase a car. First you have to deal with the salesman's game. They usually show you dozens of cars you're not even interested in. They check your credit, and then bring out tons of paperwork. Because we had tons of cash, we didn't have to go through all this bullshit.

I marched into this car dealership in New Jersey one day. After waiting around for about fifteen minutes, I got impatient. "Excuse me, can somebody help me, please?"

"Can I help you?"

"Yeah." I pointed to a car in my magazine. "I want this car right here."

The dealer looked at me like I was crazy. "Listen, son, this car doesn't go on market for another two years." With a "you-can't-afford-it" smirk on his face, he added, "Besides, buddy, that car costs a *lot* of money."

At that point, I pulled out my duffel bag, so full of crisp

hundred-dollar bills that I could barely zip it all the way across. Standing there with more than $50,000 cash, I confidently repeated myself: "I want this car right here. If you can't get it, I'll go to a dealership that can."

With a dazed look on his face, he quickly changed his tune. "Oh my! I'll see what I can do, sir. But if we can't get this car, is there another one you might be interested in? We have a nice selection of brand-new—"

"Naw, man," I interrupted. "Just get me this car."

"Okay, sir. Can you leave a phone number so we can tell you about the status of the car?" Within a week or two, the agent called me, and I returned to the dealership to pick up the hottest shit on the street. Three different salesmen—including the dealership owner himself—escorted me over to the car as if I was president of the United States. Other customers noticed the commotion, and started looking in my direction to see if I was a celebrity or something. I inspected the car thoroughly. After jumping in the driver's seat, I slowly ran my hand over the seats, and took a minute to breathe in the brand-new leather.

"All right, I'll take it."

Their faces grew excited when they saw the crisp Benjamins peacefully resting in my duffle bag. Using this method, I earned the title of being *the first person in the entire country* to own certain car models! I was only seventeen years old.

The fun thing about buying cars was customizing them, making the car your own creation. I was probably one of the first young cats to put designer rims on my cars. Now, entertainers, athletes, and street cats hook up their cars, but in the early eighties, it wasn't common.

I loved the body of a car. I would spend whatever money I needed in order to make a car look its best. I would install lambskin or butter-soft leather seats with piping in an unusual color. People may not believe it, but one of my cars had a CD player way back in the eighties!

I would cruise around Harlem feeling like a king. Usually I was a laid-back cat, but my personality changed when it came to cars. In my mind, a car should have the effect of a fine woman with a beautiful body—it should stop traffic.

Even neighborhood cops in areas where I sold drugs would stop and compliment me. It got to the point where people expected me to have the hottest car in the 'hood. Everybody wanted to know what Azie was going to pull up in next. I believed it was my personal duty to sport the hottest cars, and I never neglected that.

I often tell people that Rich, Alpo, and I were popular like the Jacksons during the eighties and nineties. We were ghetto celebrities for sure. Some idolized us, others were jealous, and some imitated us. People we didn't even know would come running up, trying to walk and talk with us. Some asked for autographs, and others wanted to take pictures with us. I'm not lying when I say we could have made good money just by charging people to take pictures next to our cars.

One day I was playing ball in the schoolyard with my boys. I saw these young cats standing around our rides taking pictures with a Polaroid camera. Then they jumped into their cars and left. Of course we were suspicious. They might have been undercover cops or carjackers. We jumped in our rides and followed the cats. I signaled the driver to pull over. When we all got out I questioned them.

"What the fuck are you doing with the camera and shit? What's that all about?"

One of them nervously replied: "Yo, man, we ain't trying to do nothing. We just love your style. Nobody in Jersey rocks cars like y'all, and we just taking pictures to show 'em how you uptown cats are living." Things like this happened all the time.

One time a Spanish hustler offered to trade four bricks of cocaine for one of my new cars. I did some quick street math: I'd paid $60,000 for the car. Four kilos of cocaine had a street value of $80,000 at the time. I made the trade and stood to earn more than $20,000 profit from the deal.

It's impossible to floss wealth without attracting envy. Jealousy is always a problem in the drug game, and it is something you must always account for and anticipate. Hot cars and iced-out jewelry drew attention and brought out the playa haters. People like this might slice your tires or run their key along the side of your car if they could get away with it. This made me very cautious about parking my cars.

I usually parked my rides in a midtown Manhattan garage or at this garage on 132nd Street. To keep cats from knowing my every move, I'd sometimes get a friend to pick up my car and drive it to the block. When I really wanted to be incognito, I rented a cab for a day or two and had the driver chauffeur me around.

By 1986, about three years into the game, I felt like Batman. I had knots of money in each pocket. My pants sagged and the crack of my ass showed from all the money I carried. At times I walked around like a fool with up to $50,000 cash. Whatever the customers paid with, I accepted, from singles to food stamps! Those were some crazy days.

The average person would be afraid to walk around with that type of money, but cats weren't trying to get at me; they were trying to get with me. Cats knew they could make some real money in my camp. Therefore, most people didn't want to shoot at me. If anything, they would jump in front of a gun and take bullets for me.

I didn't operate like a tyrant or gunslinger like many other hustlers. I didn't want cats to fear me; I wanted them to help me make money. So I never went out to recruit security. Then again, I didn't have to.

Money is powerful. When people think you can help them eat well, they will protect you. There was a chicken spot in Harlem called Bojangles where you could get biscuits that were *off the hook*! I stopped in there to buy a few every day, no matter how crowded it was. One day I was standing in line and this cat walked past the store who always made it his business to stare at me and mumble slick shit out his mouth. As he walked past, we made eye contact. Thinking aloud, I said, "Sucka-ass motherfucker."

A brother on the line in front of me whom I'd never met walked outside, brought the sucka to the window, and knocked on the glass to get my attention. When I looked, he said, "Who, him?" I didn't know what he was talking about. This cat started fucking the dude up: hooks, upper-cuts, the whole shit. He sent the cat staggering down the block, bleeding from the eye and mouth.

Keep in mind: I didn't know this dude from Adam. He introduced himself to me as Big Buck Smash. He said he was a boxer and that he heard a lot about me. He wanted to be down with my crew and handle my dirty work.

"Wow, big man . . . you are crazy," I said. In his big country voice he responded, "Naw, boss. I had an opportunity to prove myself. I'm no bullshitter, and you and I know action speaks louder than words. Well, here I am. How do you like my resume?" he asked with pride. "Did he run fast enough or should I have knocked him the fuck out?"

I told him to slow down, because I didn't like unnecessary drama. I dug in my pocket, pulled out a wad of money, and gave him about five hundred dollars. He replied, "Thank you, Big A. When I'm around, you'll never have trouble." We became cool after that.

He was about six foot five inches tall and was in excellent shape. When I met him, he wore a leather bomber and high-water slacks. He was a sight to behold! Nobody wanted to mess with Buck, though—he was quick with his tongue and even faster with his hands. He wanted a boxing career, and at one time, he sparred with former heavyweight boxing champion Larry Holmes.

One time a police officer attempted to arrest Big Buck for marijuana possession. Just as the cop was about to put the cuffs on him, Buck quickly knocked the cop out cold!

Before his partner could draw his gun, Buck knocked him the fuck out too, and then took off running down the block! It seemed like the entire police force was after him in hot pursuit. When he ran to a secluded area they shot at him and told him to freeze.

When I asked why he stopped, he replied, "When I heard that gunshot, I realized I could die. I don't care how fast or strong you are; no man wants to die. I can get knocked the fuck out and get back up but when you get shot only a chosen few return . . . and Big Buck wasn't taking no chances," he said with a hearty laugh.

"I stopped at the drop of dime when I heard that gun," Buck continued. "I paid for running, though. While one officer put the cuffs on, the others beat my ass with black-jacks. They bust my head wide open! I was alone in the backseat of the cop car and my head hurt like crazy, but I started thinking, 'Damn, I just knocked out two of New York City's finest!'

"I started to panic when I thought those cops might kill me when we got to the precinct. I wasn't gonna let that shit happen, so I kicked the door open and took off running again like Carl Lewis."

I couldn't believe it. It sounded like something from a movie. It must have been a crazy sight seeing Big Buck run from the cops with his hands behind his back and his knees hitting him in the face. According to Buck, an officer tripped him up with a nightstick and Buck went tumbling over like a tall tree chopped down by a lumber-jack. I asked, "Why did you run?" "I saw Burt Reynolds do it in a movie," he replied. Buck was a crazy dude, a real Richard Pryor. Crazy shit like that always went down in the 'hood.

After fucking with Big Buck, I jumped into my UFO and pulled off. I always used to ride with my little man Whip. He was my right-hand man, like Robin the Boy Wonder. Whip always talked shit when we rolled: "Yeah, yeah, yeah, y'all see it's real!" "More to come, niggers!" "We just getting started; warming up!" "Yo! None of y'all cats can fuck with my crew, we doing it for real!"

I felt like nothing could stop us. We were young king-pins getting a lot of cash. Our notoriety spread throughout the 'hood and we became ghetto celebrities. Everybody and their mother visited our headquarters on 132nd Street and Seventh Avenue.

My man Chuck from Mount Vernon brought LL Cool J around several times. Big Mike from Queens brought Salt-N-Pepa through many times. Other celebrity visitors included Heavy D and the Boyz, Roxanne Shanté, Keith Sweat, Red Alert, Luvbug Starski, Treach from Naughty by Nature, Biz Markie, Puffy, Chuck Chillout, Mr. Magic, Al B. Sure!, Eric B. and Rakim, DJ Hollywood, and my man Busy motherfuckin' Bee.

Although I hustled, I tried to steer young cats away from that life. I did it to survive and get ahead. But I always encouraged younger dudes to leave the drug hustle alone, especially if they had other things going on for themselves. There were plenty of times when I sent young cats away and told them to stay in school. I refused to deprive cats of their middle or high school education just to hustle on the streets.

Game Over

I remember a young brother named Teddy who lived right down the block from my headquarters. He had skills when it came to producing music. One time he asked me for some work; he wanted to hustle. I told him to stick with his music, because hustling wasn't for him. I'm glad he followed his dream. Teddy Riley went on to produce successful groups like Guy and Blackstreet. He created a new sound called New Jack Swing in the eighties and nineties, and became the musical force behind a number of R&B and pop hits.

Paid in Full

I always wanted to see people in my neighborhood eat and have fun. My crew threw bus rides, and anyone around the way could go for free. We went to places like Wildwood Water Park, Great Adventure, and Rye Playland. Something about seeing the neighborhood kids enjoying themselves did something to me.

We regularly sponsored block parties and Christmas parties. I paid the legendary DJ Hollywood and DJ Grand Chaka to do the music, and they always had the parties jumping. Usually we sponsored talent shows at these parties, so local kids had a chance to shine. We might have a singing, dance, or rap contest. Everyone left with a prize like motor scooters, ten-speed bikes, or a few hundred dollars. We even raffled three or four hundred dollars to the adults. Toward the end of the party when I had to roll out, I always threw five hundred singles up in the air for the kids.

Me and the fellas played basketball for big money during our downtime. Zip, John-John, Chubby, Alfonzo, Buford, Tuffy, The Chief, and Little Mike Boogie were always ready for action on the court, and we had mad fun. Cats like Prince and Big Mike from Queens traveled all the way uptown to ball with us. We always had intense games with those Queens cats.

When it came to ball, I didn't care what the bets were; I took them all and had fun, win or lose. If I lost, I always paid, with no arguments or bullshit. My philosophy was that money didn't make me; I made money.

Sometimes we watched games at the famous Rucker's Basketball Tournament held in Rucker's park. Holcombe Rucker, a parks and recreation worker, started the tournament in the sixties to prevent kids from falling victim to the streets. His motto was "Each One Teach One." Players like Earl "The Goat" Manigault, Julius "Dr. J" Erving, Nate "Tiny" Archibald, and Pee Wee Kirkland all earned reputations on the Rucker court.

Plenty of cats playing ball in the 'hood have potential to play professional ball. Joe Hammond was one of those cats. Joe Hammond was a street basketball legend with good handle, ups, and speed. Joe's legend as a street baller rose when he dropped sixty-two points on Julius "Dr. J" Irving in front of a sold-out crowd at Rucker park. In fact, Joe played Lakers' great Jerry West one-on-one and beat him!

Joe once told me that he turned down a contract to play with the Los Angeles Lakers back in the seventies because he "made more money selling heroin in one month than he could make playing pro ball in a year." The streets called, and the Lakers called, but I guess the streets spoke louder. He regrets answering that call to this day.

When I speak to youth, the one question they always ask is "How much money did you make?" On average, at the top of my game I pulled in about $40,000 a week profit back in the mid-eighties. On days like Christmas or New Year's I always made more because people liked to get fucked up during the holidays. I made $50,000 one Christmas Eve. The following New Year's Eve I made a $70,000 profit.

The largest profit I earned in one day was about $150,000, and I'll never forget how it happened. I was walking into Lenox Terrace, and I noticed a well-dressed African brother approaching me. Moments before I'd noticed that the Mercedes-Benz he drove had diplomatic plates.

"Are you Azie?"

"No. Who wants to know?"

"Don't worry," he said. "I'm not the law."

After checking him out for a minute, we started talking business. This cat gave me a hundred bricks to sell, which took me several weeks. I made more than a million dollars off that deal alone.

Most of my money didn't come from one-shot deals. I had several locations in the hood: 132nd Street and Seventh Avenue; 145th Street between Seventh and Eighth Avenues, up on Sugar Hill; 130th Street between Lenox and Fifth Avenues; and 134th Street between Seventh and Lenox. Each spot pulled in a $10,000 profit a week, which was big money back in the eighties.

Game Over

I supplied each spot with the product, and helped the workers establish clientele. To be honest, though, Lulu's product basically sold itself. You might have heard the saying "Good dope sells itself." That's a fact. I collected my money from each spot every week. I established other "chiefs" instead of trying to run everything myself, and I shared my profit.

A lot of cats thought they were working for me, but I made bosses, not workers. I constantly had to remind cats that they worked for themselves. I was no slave owner. I was in pursuit of making money to help support *my* family, *my* wants, and *my* needs. I got a package from Lulu, but I set my own prices and bottled the coke up the way I wanted. I worked for myself. If the police ever busted my operation, it wouldn't be Lulu's responsibility; it would be mine. I wanted anyone who was down with me to adopt the same thinking.

They would break the coke down by putting it into perfume sample bottles, which held about 0.8 of a gram to one gram. You can get a thousand bottles or better from a kilo of uncut coke depending on whether the coke is heavy or light. I always had the light, fluffy, fish scale–pure cocaine.

A bottle usually sold for $50, but I changed that. Bottles went from $50 to $40 to $30 to $20, then $10, until there was no competition in my view. We had quantity and quality. The whole 'hood was getting money. We cornered the market.

My road to wealth basically worked like this: I received a kilo from Lulu for the cheap price of $10,000. I sold the kilo for $15,000, so I made $5,000 off every kilo. A dude could take that same kilo, break it down into bottles, and make about $40,000 in the streets. From that $25,000 profit, he paid his workers and himself. This method allowed me to get rid of tons of coke fast. Lulu got his money on time, the customers got high at good cost, and I got paid—everybody involved was happy and satisfied.

Soon, other dealers from Manhattan, the Bronx, Brooklyn, and Queens began coming to me because my coke was so pure and cheap. I guess you can say I took the coke game from retail to wholesale. I also took coke out of the bars and clubs and began pitching it on street corners, building lobbies, and eventually actual drug spots. My formula prevented me from taking a loss because I always got my money right off the top. Since I didn't do much hand-to-hand sales, I also was able to keep a low profile from the cops.

After establishing a spot that could move two kilos a week, these cats would purchase their product at wholesale prices and break it down on the street level. This is how I made $40,000-a-week profit (by making $5,000 off each kilo).

Before the eighties cocaine was considered a rich man's high. It used to sell for $100 a gram, and you usually bought it in the local bars or you could get it from the Dominicans who sold it in certain apartments off the scale. There was another spot on 147th Street and St. Nicholas Avenue called 6250 where you could purchase a gram for $62.50. That coke was cut, meaning that it was mixed with lactose to stretch the profit; but it made the "medicine" weak. As a result, customers got a weaker high for their money.

I was lucky. Lulu had a direct line to the Colombian cocaine kingpin Pablo Escobar. There were no middlemen involved. Therefore, I was able to get the best product at the lowest prices. I paid so little per kilo that I didn't have to dilute the coke to make money. This meant I could sell undiluted coke at the cheapest prices and still make a big profit. My position in the game was serious. I gave my customers the best product at the lowest prices.

What happened if a cat ran off or didn't pay me? I never used a gun to shoot, kill, or threaten anybody. Gun play just wasn't a part of my repertoire. If a cat didn't have my money, I just never fucked with them again. They never had the opportunity to make money with anybody associated with me.

In the drug game, being without a supplier was like being without blood; you can't survive without it. Most people knew I was the dude to fuck with if you wanted the best product to make some real paper. I had a lot of power, but I never used or attempted to use it for war. People did not want to betray my trust or lose my love.

Most of the time, I never had to worry about someone not paying me, because I knew who to fuck with and who not to fuck with. I knew the lions, the wolves, sharks, and the snakes. And I always tried to keep the kings of the jungle around me who also knew the wolves, sharks, and the snakes.

Lulu was my first and major cocaine connection. As time went on, my reputation for selling weight quickly spread in the streets. Believe it or not, drug connects began looking for *me*, asking me to push their product! They would give me free samples of coke as a way of persuading me to work with them. Sometimes I got an eighth of a kilo or more, which of course I sold. I usually sold my free sample for about $4,000, which I used to purchase the hottest rims for one of my exotic rides. These free samples were basically free money. Sometimes a connect made me an offer I couldn't refuse, but for the most part, I stayed loyal to my man Lulu.

The majority of the new connects wanted me to sell crack because in their eyes, crack seemed to move quicker than coke. Crack, or freebase, is a form of cocaine melted down to oil, hardened by ice water, and cooked with baking soda. Now it's at the purest form and ready to smoke. Crack does more damage than an atomic bomb: crack babies, robbing your own family, violence, prostitution, etc.

When crack first popped on the scene in Harlem, there was this crack house—a private house called 404 where people stayed all day and night getting high. That spot sold huge garbage pails of crack. When they got busted by the law they got right out with no case because the labs tested the crack and it showed up as baking soda. It was actually legit to sell crack for about a year before the law figured it out.

I deeply believe that's how crack spread like wildfire, because cats could initially sell it without fear of doing time. Today, you can get lots of time for selling crack or having it in your possession. By the time law enforcement caught on, the damage was done. Many were hooked, users *and* sellers. Big money was involved. If I had any knowledge about the stock market back then, I would have invested in Arm & Hammer Baking Soda! Crack sales in the United States had to make their stock go through the roof in the eighties. Damn, that's why knowledge is the key.

Crack was popular with hustlers and customers for a few reasons: Dealers found they could sell crack extremely cheap and make a huge profit; and crack addicts, or "crackheads," loved the drug because it gave them a quick and intense high for a fraction of what coke cost.

Because Rich sold crack, most people assumed I did too. However, this is not true. I never dealt crack one day in my life, only pure cocaine. Both crack and cocaine are poison, but my decision to stay away from crack was financial, not moral. The process of making crack wasted too much time for me. Why cook when I can just bottle and sell?

There are different ways to use cocaine: you can sniff it, heat it up and inject it, or smoke it. By selling cocaine in powder form, I could sell my product to the greatest number of people. Bottom line: I made more money than the crack dealer, who could only sell to people who smoked crack. Besides, when you cook cocaine into crack, you're doing the crackhead's job. If the nigga wants to cook his coke, let him do it himself. My goal was to sell the coke as quickly as possible . . . pure cocaine. From there, a cat could do what they wanted to do with it. My decision to stay away from crack and just deal with cocaine was an intelligent business decision.

It may sound shocking to have me associate intelligence

with drug dealing. People usually associate intelligence with being a lawyer, doctor, or professor. But the truth is, a dumb person can't succeed in anything. Even criminals must make intelligent decisions in order to prosper. This is why I never kept large amounts of drugs and money in the same place. If I ever got busted, the cops could never take my drugs *and* money. Rather than pushing coke on the streets, I tried to wholesale it so I could be behind the scenes, or as the streets would say, "Stay low."

Most of all, I stayed away from the spotlight. In my business, being seen was a bad thing. I just wanted to make money. I didn't want to be famous or popular. Why? Because almost every criminal I know who became famous and popular was murdered, usually by people they knew. I was already known in the streets, but I didn't want to attract any unnecessary attention.

I'm not arrogant or foolish. There were many cats dealing drugs in Harlem and throughout America. A lot of dudes made money in the drug game. But I'm one of the few that avoided death and incarceration. That was mostly through God's grace, but the way I operated had something to do with it too. "Eat and let eat" was my motto. As I would learn much later, God's grace would help me survive the most tragic experience in my life.

Married to the Mob

In my experience, women want to feel comfortable and protected. They also like nice things. It's in their nature to strive for the best. The queen wants to be with the king. Ladies in the game want furs, diamonds, cars, the latest hairdo, and designer bags like Gucci and Fendi. When women choose to deal with street dudes to get these types of presents, they are married to the mob, like it or not. You are the company you keep.

Men in the game seek the most beautiful women in the 'hood. The king wants to be with the queen. It's the law of nature. Some women start off innocent, but circumstances and the hypnosis of bling bling cause them to go astray. Women in the game usually seek out the boss or the toughest and richest guy on the streets. Every Bonnie wants a Clyde and every Clyde wants a Bonnie.

I've heard many stories about the groupies, or obsessed female fans of athletes and entertainers. These women wait backstage or in hotel lobbies day and night, hoping for a chance to meet and sleep with their idols. Successful hustlers also have groupies. Our power and wealth came from selling drugs as opposed to scoring baskets or singing pretty songs, but the bottom line is that some women are attracted to men with power and wealth. Once women in the 'hood knew about the huge knots of money we had and the hot cars we drove, it was just a matter of time before they became our "fans."

I can say from experience—and with no exaggeration—that many young ladies were willing to satisfy all of a street hustler's sexual fantasies if doing so allowed them to purchase clothes, get their hair and nails done, wear expensive jewelry, or pay their bills. We had an understanding: They provided the sex, and we provided the gifts. Many so-called respectable women have a similar understanding with men. In return for sexual favors and their time, these women expect men to lavish them with vacations, houses, expensive jewelry, and cash. As you can see, the hustle doesn't change, just the gifts involved.

I don't want people to misunderstand me. If two people are in a committed relationship, they should expect to support each other financially, spiritually, and otherwise. Gold digging is all about using someone to meet your material needs only. This type of relationship is always shallow, but at least it is fair when both parties get what they want.

Sometimes the gold-digging game got ridiculous and downright tacky. Grown men would approach me with their own sister's phone number, telling me how much their sister wanted to meet me. In these cases, the sister expected me to shower her with money or presents, and her brother figured I owed him a favor for setting me up with his sister.

One time a dirty cop gave me his sister's number and damn near begged me to call her. I did, and we arranged to go out on a date. During dinner, she reached into her purse and pulled out two pictures: one of a fur coat and one of a car. With a devilish smile, she told me, "This is what I want for Christmas." Thinking to myself, "This bitch must be crazy," I simply laughed it off. Here it is our first date, and she was already hitting me up for presents! I decided to teach her a lesson. On our next date, I gave her a picture I'd ripped from a porno magazine. It showed a woman on her knees, giving one man a blowjob, with another guy hitting it from behind. With a wicked smile, I said, "This is what *I* want for Christmas!" She was offended, but I did make a point. I wasn't sure what she heard about me, but I was no dummy.

Sometimes my street status caused sex to just fall into my lap without me having to do much work. One time I was on the first-floor staircase of a building waiting for my man to make a coke sale on the second floor. An attractive older woman, maybe in her thirties, came from her apartment wearing a revealing sundress.

She noticed me sitting there and commented that she knew who I was. I just sat there, quietly undressing her with my eyes. She said, "I see you checking me out. I know you want some of this." Before I could reply, she lifted her dress, started touching herself, and eventually straddled me right there on the staircase. After our encounter, she gave me her number and told me to stay in touch.

Another time I was chillin' by headquarters on 132nd Street when a cute girl came up to the stoop and started the familiar small-talk routine: "I know who you are, heard a lot about you," etc. Within minutes—I kid you not—the girl got on her knees, unzipped my jeans, and gave me head right there in broad daylight.

Incidents like this were exceptional; most of the time I did have to do some work to pull off a sexual adventure. Even in those times, the women usually approached me first. My man and I stopped in this Caribbean restaurant in Harlem called the Hot Pot one evening. A beautiful waitress came to me asking if I was "the famous Azie." I lied just to get her out of my face so I could eat. My friend couldn't believe it.

"What the fuck is wrong with you, man? That fine bitch is tryin' to hit on you, and you here playing shy? You need to stop bullshittin' and tell her who you are so we can all fuck tonight!"

The girl came back with a sexy smirk on her face.

"Yes you are . . . you are Azie!"

This time I told the truth and asked what her plans were for the evening.

"Me and my girlfriend are about to get off. We're down to hang wit' y'all if that's cool."

Later that evening, I bought some liquor and rented two hotel rooms. The girls were tipsy and horny within thirty minutes. The liquor had them talking shit about how good they were in bed, and about all the freaky shit they were going to do.

My friend saw it was time to get busy so he got up and gestured for the other waitress to follow him to the other room. He gave me that "I'm about to fuck the shit out of her" wink, and proceeded out the door. The young lady followed but closed and locked the door behind my man. I was shocked. She turned to me and made her intentions *real* clear:

"Look, Azie, I don't know that nigga; I'm trying to fuck *you*."

My friend probably spent the entire night watching television and listening to our threesome, long into the night. The girls must've done their porno movie homework, because they did everything in the book. While I satisfied one, they satisfied each other.

The next morning my angry friend banged on the door and demanded me to dismiss the chicks. I did what any brother would've done in that situation: I dismissed *him* and continued having fun with the ladies.

These stories of my sexual encounters reflect the way I viewed women during my hustling days. I'm not the same man anymore, so the same things don't appeal to me. At the same time, I don't feel that I owe an apology to anyone except Pat.

Pat loved me and I loved her back. However, I did cheat on her back in the day. She was by my side way before all the money, cars, and jewelry. I trusted her and still do. She is my heart to this day.

I don't know any man who shares Pat's strength—not

physical, but emotional and psychological. Pat experienced unbelievable tragedies and still held her head up. She gets nothing but love from me, and I'll love her forever. For all it's worth, I deeply regret cheating on Pat and violating her trust.

As for the other women I dealt with, I apologize for any pain or false hopes I created. The truth is that I never lied to these women. They all knew I was not about to leave Pat for them. Women on the side knew that our relationship was strictly based on friendship and that I had no intention of committing to them.

Not that these women necessarily wanted a commitment either. My hustle was coke, and their hustle was sex. Women involved with cats in the drug game typically provide sex in exchange for money. The majority of the women I dealt with made that point clear. Only foolish brothers would mistake their freakiness for love.

I knew women who would wear a sexy outfit to catch a certain guy's eye at a party. They would stay with that guy long enough to get money, jewelry, and additional clothes. The next week they would use those same clothes to catch a new guy, and the cycle would begin again. Hustlers were out to get the baddest chick, and women in the game were out to get the hustler with the most money. That's just how the game went down. There was no morality involved, just pleasure and convenience.

I don't hate on women. I recognize the difference between good women and those who are only out for themselves, or gold diggers. I don't treat a hoe like a housewife, nor do I treat a strong sister like a bimbo. My interaction with a woman comes from how that woman conducts herself. It is also important to note that not all the women I encountered were gold-digging hoes. Some held regular jobs, were educated, and were basically decent people.

Some women were attracted to my personality and my vibe. For them, money was not an issue. I remember one woman who constantly urged me to invest my money in legitimate business ventures and stocks. I also had a number of women who were just platonic friends—no sex was involved, and no intention to have sex was involved. We could laugh and talk about life just like regular friends.

My street experiences caused me to be suspicious of women. I probably misjudged some truly good sisters due to baggage I carried from past situations. I had to learn to distinguish good sisters from the hoes and users.

If I'm with a woman, I give her my all. If I come and dump $1,000 on the table, I don't see it as *my* money, but *our* money. The money will go toward taking care of *our* home. But the woman should also come and put her money on the table. If she wants me to produce money and sees herself as being entitled to it, then she can't secretly stash her money and keep it for herself. That violates the trust, and that's not how I operate. Once the trust is punctured, the relationship is dead.

I'd like to think I'm straightforward; I keep no secrets. I'm fair and generous. But if I go around expecting some female or some cat to operate like me, I'll be disappointed forever. I've learned that you can't go through life mindful of only your own values. You must know the rules and values of the people you deal with too.

Game Over

It took me some time to address how I used money to fulfill my lust for women. "Damn, she looks good; let me go get the Benz and get fresh to pull this chick." That's how I used to be. I had shallow connections and low regard for women, then wondered why I couldn't be in a meaningful relationship years later.

Now I know it is impossible to find the right woman if you attract her with material shit. This is something I struggled with for a long time, and it's something I still work on. I want to murder that trait in myself that makes me use money and gifts to attract a woman.

A book woke me up to what love really means. *Angel's Guide* by Belinda Womack says that you can't love anyone until you love yourself. Just because a man wants to make love doesn't mean he loves a woman. True love, when two people's thoughts and spirits connect, is so much deeper than a lust-driven flesh connection. As I matured, I realized that true relationships involve trust, respect, sacrifice, and commitment.

Women who are married to the mob view themselves as sexual objects and project themselves that way. These sisters need to understand that a woman is so much more. People like Harriet Tubman and Sojourner Truth fought against racism and enslavement at a time when black people—especially women—had few resources. Many present-day households, businesses, schools, churches, and community organizations would not survive were it not for the vision and strength of women.

8
Lifestyles of the Rich and Infamous

I've always been a quick learner, and I learned a lot in my life, though not from formal schooling. Much of my lessons came from living and observing. Every nation in the world has poor people. In fact, poor people make up the majority of the world's population. Even America, the richest, most powerful nation on Earth, has millions of poor people.

Most people believe that the civil rights movement and Martin Luther King, Jr., ended segregation in the United States. Honestly speaking, American neighborhoods are still separated according to race and income. Most times, the rich want to live far away from the poor. They want to ignore how "the other people live."

Well-off people are often afraid that living close to poor people might result in their "goodies" being stolen.

Game Over

To avoid uncomfortable situations like guilt and theft, the rich live in exclusive, remote neighborhoods, far away from the have-nots.

Physical distance, however, can no longer entirely separate the rich from the poor. Technology—in the form of television, movies, and the Internet—makes the world smaller. The government worries about nations spying on them. But average citizens can use the Internet to find all types of underground information in a matter of minutes! You can even look up criminal records on the Internet.

Teenagers in Japan wear the same hip-hop fashions as New York's urban youth, and Eastern Europeans are now familiar with Brooklyn slang. In time, people around the world might come to respect all cultures. Of course, the smaller world created by technology has a negative effect also: Thanks to the Internet and television, the poor know how rich people dress, what nightspots they go to, where they purchase jewelry from, and what cars they drive. Now, more than ever, poor people feel the pressure to live like rich people.

When I was growing up, a TV show called *Lifestyles of the Rich and Famous* exposed many poor people to the glamour of wealthy living: private jets, solid gold knives and forks, twenty-room mansions, and so forth. I saw an episode that featured Morris the cat, the famous cat from the old Nine Lives cat food commercials. This cat had a sixty-three-room mansion and his own chauffeur-driven Rolls Royce. I'm sure he made his mother and father very proud of him! Meanwhile, in my 'hood, countless homeless people searched through garbage cans for food.

Lifestyles of the Rich and Infamous

Poor people saw things on that show that they could only dream about. Very few poor people I knew criticized the waste and vanity of the people highlighted on the show. Instead, we envied the rich, and craved to experience their lifestyles even more. These days MTV has a show called *MTV Cribs*, in which famous entertainers show off their homes and cars. This show has an even more powerful influence than *Lifestyles* because young people relate to many of the entertainers featured.

Television shows like the ones I mentioned seem entertaining, but they shit on poor people. There I am, wondering where my next meal is coming from, and I see some rich guy being served by his personal chef aboard a private jet. You're living in some overcrowded, roach-infested studio apartment, watching how some singer has just installed a remote-controlled waterfall in her living room. These things can eat at a person's pride after a while.

In a world where money is king, being poor made me feel unimportant as a child. No one wants to feel unimportant. Since poor people have no material wealth, they lust for things that make them appear wealthy and successful. Scholars call these things "status symbols."

This explains why people living on public assistance or welfare—in dirty living conditions, with roaches and mice eating better than they do—spend what little money they have on sneakers, clothes, jewelry, hairstyles, and manicures. They want to look and feel like a million bucks in a nation that makes them feel like shit.

Growing up, I knew some parents who were embarrassed to send their children to school dressed in hand-me-down clothes. However, some of those same parents had no problem sending their children to school hungry.

This crazy set of priorities is not just an issue for poor people; members of the middle and upper class are guilty also. We have all heard stories about athletes or entertainers with million-dollar contracts who went broke within a few years. The bottom line is they are not used to having anything, and they suffer from low self-esteem. Being poor made them feel powerless and unimportant. Wealth gives them the chance to feel powerful. Therefore, they run out and spend their way to feeling important, then flaunt their wealth to feel even better.

I understand the "rags to riches" thing, because I went through it. I was a poor kid who grew up on welfare, wore hand-me-down clothes, and got teased in school. I remember feeling miserable. I resented my poor background and the fact that I couldn't "shine" like other kids.

I did not have many opportunities to "make it." I can truthfully say I didn't know anyone my age who became successful by going to school and landing a good job. Unfortunately, I did have access to drugs. I knew plenty of people who sold it, and I lived in a neighborhood where drug dealers were as common as blades of grass in a park.

I wish I could say that religion or some political movement inspired me at a young age. The truth is that selling drugs changed my life. Cocaine became my hustle when I was a teenager. It was my bread and butter, and my temporary ticket out of poverty.

It seemed like I went from welfare to wealthy in six seconds. As anyone in that situation can relate to, my partners and I spent money like crazy. Once money started rolling in, we wanted to sample the lifestyles of the rich and famous.

Today we see rappers flaunting extravagant jewelry covered with expensive diamonds. Flashy jewelry is now common in hip-hop culture, but I believe we started that trend in the early eighties. I'm not proud of that fact, but it's true.

I was never much of a jewelry fanatic, but I did buy a few nice chains and medallions. I bought most of my jewelry in midtown Manhattan's Diamond District, around 47th Street and Sixth Avenue. A jeweler on Canal Street made a lot of my customized jewelry too.

Usually, I tried to make my jewelry match the car I wanted to drive at the time. For instance, when I bought my BMW 735 (known as the 7) I sported a gold number 7 flooded with diamonds. It cost me about $12,000. When I bought my first Benz, I wore a Benz car medallion that had more ice than a freezer. I had another medallion featuring a top hat, white gloves, and cane to represent a gentleman. Most medallions I owned cost between $10,000 and $20,000, but we bought them like socks back then.

Rich and Alpo wore expensive jewelry too. Rich would wear something simple like a gold and diamond ring or a gold watch. However, that ring and watch cost more than some people made all year. Alpo had rings custommade to fit over four fingers. He had one ring like this that spelled out his name in diamonds. It resembled a very fancy set of brass knuckles, and there was talk in the streets that such rings were illegal because of this. To my knowledge, Alpo was the first cat to rock a four-finger ring. The next thing you know, rap artists like LL Cool J and Biz Markie began wearing four-finger rings too.

A street hustler lives a fast-paced, hectic life. Everything and everybody moves one thousand miles an hour in the drug game, and you must always be alert. A hustler needs a safe, quiet place to come home to, where he can relax and recharge his batteries for the next day. Jewelry and cars were luxuries, but apartments and houses were necessities in the game. They provided a place to rest, store drugs, count money, and entertain female guests.

Since Harlem was my stomping ground, I rented apartments in the Riverbend and Lenox Terrace Complexes. When I was younger, only well-off blacks lived in those apartment complexes. When I moved in, I had a feeling of success, like I had "made it."

Lenox Terrace is located right on 135th Street between Lenox and Fifth Avenues. Nearby were the Harlem YMCA, Harlem Hospital, the Schomburg Library, Pan Pan's Diner, a Parks and Recreation Center nicknamed The Bath House, and the 2 train. On any given day, you could find drug dealers, doctors, teachers, street vendors, street-corner preachers, drug addicts, ball players, and homeless people in the neighborhood.

Lenox Terrace was also an ideal location because it put me close to my drug headquarters on 132nd Street and Seventh Avenue. Riverbend Apartments is located right by the 138th Street Bridge that connects Harlem to the Bronx. I assume it was named Riverbend because it overlooked the Harlem River. My Harlem apartments were my good-time spots; places I took women when it was time to freak off. For security reasons, I never actually slept in those apartments.

According to street rules, you should never shit where you eat. If you do business where you rest, you make yourself a target for jealous cats and criminals; the chaos of the streets sneaks up into your home. Since I sold drugs in Harlem, I bought places in New Jersey and Long Island where I could actually rest and lay low.

I owned two properties in New Jersey. I purchased a condominium in an exclusive complex called The Galaxy, located in Guttenberg, New Jersey. The property cost about $125,000 and it had a beautiful view overlooking the Hudson River. The actress Brooke Shields and former New York Yankee outfielder Ricky Henderson were my neighbors, although we didn't know each other.

I also bought a traditional house in Teaneck, New Jersey, that cost $260,000. I decked the house out in Persian rugs, huge floor-model televisions in every room, and plush leather furniture. I bought the house for my mother.

The goal was to move my mom out of the 'hood, and into a beautiful house in a quiet and safe part of town. I gave the Realtor a huge down payment and set it up so my mother's mortgage payments were equal to the rent she paid for her little apartment in Harlem. I think every son dreams of growing up to buy his mom a house.

Unfortunately, my mother refused to move in. She knew I sold drugs, and probably heard about some of the dangerous cats I chilled with. After I was attacked in

1987, she was scared to death. She always assumed that lightning might strike twice, and that if it did, anyone standing by me would be hit too. She wanted to avoid the electrocution. She said she would not be able to enjoy the house, and refused to view it. She begged me to sell it and give her the money. When she refused to move in, I made it one of my properties. My mother never came to visit me there.

My favorite property was a duplex condominium in Freeport, Long Island, that cost $210,000. It had the makings of an official bachelor pad: a heated pool, a two-car garage, a spiral staircase that led from the living room to the master bedroom, a dishwasher, and a washer and dryer for my clothes. The neighborhood was predominantly white with a little sprinkle of black residents.

I was always on the go, so I never stayed in one house for too long. The white residents didn't see me often, but I often wondered what they would do if they knew a cocaine dealer lived in their 'hood.

I bought these properties to provide refuge from the bullshit I had to deal with in the drug game. I wanted peace, quiet, and relaxation. Unfortunately, the nature of my business made it impossible for me to relax even in the most luxurious homes. Drug dealing caused paranoia to invade my mind. Damn near everybody became my potential murderer or prosecutor. My heart jumped around like a break dancer whenever I heard an ambulance or saw a police car. Even though I tasted the "American Dream," living illegally made it a nightmare for me.

I often hear young brothers in the drug game talk about

how they don't worry about being arrested or being killed by rival drug dealers. I usually smile to myself when I hear such bullshit. A hustler has one goal in mind: to make as much money as possible without being caught. Imprisonment or death defeats that purpose, so they are the two things all criminals fear. When you hear hustlers say that don't fear prison or death, *they are lying*. If no one feared death or prison, gun and ammunition manufacturers, along with bodyguards, would be out of business.

One time I left my house in New Jersey. In rushing out of the house, I left $110,000 on the bed and a loaded gun on the couch. It didn't help that I also left my stereo system blasting. When I returned later, my stereo system was off. I quickly ran over to the couch and saw my gun was where I left it. Then it hit me: "They took my money!" I sprinted to my bedroom and to my surprise, found all my money there. A dozen scenarios ran through my head: "Was it the feds? Was somebody checking out my crib, preparing to rob it?" I went down to the management office for some answers:

"Yo, who was in my crib?" The guy didn't understand my slang.

"Uh, your crib?"

"My house, motherfucka!"

"Oh, I'm sorry, sir. The neighbors complained that your music was too loud."

"So people can just key into my private property anytime they want to?"

"Sir, people pay a lot of money to live here, and they expect peace and quiet when they come home."

I grew more upset with every syllable that came out of the guy's mouth.

"I pay a lot of money too, and I expect privacy. Don't go in my fucking crib again!"

I tried my best to stay under control. I knew I was fighting a losing battle. They probably saw the money and the gun. For all I knew, they'd contacted the police. I removed all the guns and money from the house after that incident. Every time I walked in the building, I felt that all eyes were on me—or maybe it was just my paranoia. Not long afterward, I sold that property.

Cars, jewelry, and nice houses are key ingredients in flossing, or showing off your wealth. Hustlers also did this by maintaining a nice wardrobe. I must admit that I wasn't the most fashionable cat in the 'hood. My idea of fashion was a T-shirt, sneakers or boots, and jeans.

Rich, on the other hand, was always sharp. Although he dressed casually, he always wore high-quality, expensive clothes. He never came out looking sloppy; the brother was extremely neat and clean. I never saw him wear an outfit twice.

Since we all wanted to stand out from everyone else, we had some of our clothes tailored. Back in the eighties, we went to a popular tailor shop in Harlem called Dapper Dan's on 125th Street and Madison Avenue. Dan made his living by purchasing authentic fabrics from top designers like Gucci, MCM, and Louis Vuitton, and creating custom-made coats, jackets, baseball caps, pants, and suits that the original designer didn't even make. If you bought something from Dan, you knew it was one of a kind. Alpo wore a few Gucci and MCM suits, and we all had—believe this or not—Gucci bulletproof vests!

We influenced hip-hop clothing in the same way we influenced hip-hop car buying and jewelry. Look at old pictures of rappers in the eighties. They came from Brooklyn, Queens, Long Island, and the Bronx. You will notice them wearing outfits and accessories from Dapper Dan's shop. Harlem drug dealers like us exposed them to his Harlem shop.

Although I had crazy money, I was never able to go on a nice vacation. The drug game was too hectic for that. I was always on the go, taking care of business. Taking too much of a break meant lost opportunities to make paper. I rarely even attended parties in the 'hood. The last thing I wanted to do was attract attention to myself. Besides, I hated to be around phony-ass people. For this reason, I stayed away from parties and huge social events the way a Muslim stays away from a pork chop.

The only party I remember attending was Alpo's birthday party one year, and that was because he begged me to go. I showed my face, we drank some Moët and Cristal, and then we took pictures. I broke out not long after I arrived; I had to get out of those tight-ass shoes!

Alpo was my social opposite. He loved being the center of attention and the subject of discussion. Alpo damn near lived at the Rooftop. The Rooftop attracted a young, wild crowd, which resulted in several robberies, shootings, and murders.

I never understood why Alpo or any hustler wanted to chill in a club like that. Why go to a spot full of rival dealers who might be jealous of you? Why put yourself in the line of fire just to show off? Most of the hustlers in the Rooftop went to show off their cars, clothes, women, and jewelry. It was a big competition.

Places like the Rooftop made things easier for the cops. Hundreds of New York City's most wanted drug dealers and other local criminals socialized in the club every week. It provided cops with a one-stop arresting place every weekend. Cops showed their appreciation by routinely harassing and sometimes arresting every hustler they could. I used to beg Alpo not to go. I told him it was too hot, and would draw too much attention. However, 'Po loved being on stage.

Drug dealers on the paper chase don't have much time to relax. When I had time to chill, I listened to music. They say that music tames the savage beast. I believe this, because music helped me escape the craziness going on around me. Rap was growing strong back then and I would cruise through Harlem in my latest ride, pumping the music of my favorite artists. Back then, I listened to Eric B. and Rakim, KRS-One, Public Enemy, and Kool G Rap.

I liked rappers who kicked truth about the streets and about life. To me, their music was real. "Move the Crowd," "Paid in Full," "Follow the Leader," "Ghetto," and "The Microphone Fiend Rakim" established Rakim as the greatest lyricist—in my opinion—of all time.

KRS-One and his DJ, Scott La Rock, produced some crazy joints too. The *Criminal Minded* album was crazy when it dropped. *My Philosophy* was tough too. My favorite KRS joint was "Still Number 1." My man KRS is a bad boy! Chuck D., Flavor Flav, and Public Enemy were off the chain too! I felt that album *It Takes a Nation of Millions to Hold Us Back*. Some of my favorite songs were "Don't Believe the Hype," "Black Steel in the Hour of Chaos," "Welcome to the Terrordome," and "Fight the Power."

The streets felt Kool G Rap because he spoke to street issues. He had this one joint called "The Streets of New York," and another called "Road to Riches." He made this song called "Rikers Island" that was the first hardcore rap song I ever heard played on the radio. I can't forget people like MC Shan and Marley Marl. Shan made "The Bridge," "I Pioneered This," and "Kill that Noise." I thought his delivery was mad smooth. None of these dudes were your average rap artists. All these cats had knowledge of self. They weren't just rapping; they were teaching and uplifting people.

To be honest, rap was too hot to hold in the eighties. I could name a whole list of cats who rocked the mic back then, and they all had different styles: Doug E. Fresh and Slick Rick, Big Daddy Kane, Kool Moe Dee, Chubb Rock, EPMD . . . I had all their music pumping in my rides. I liked cats from the West Coast too. NWA, the Geto Boys, and Snoop all got much play from me. My man Dr. Dre was and is one of the best producers ever. His *Chronic* album was off the hook.

Thanks to MTV, I listened to a few white boys too, like Phil Collins and Peter Gabriel. Collins's "In the Air Tonight" and "It's Gonna Get Better" are two of my favorite songs to this day. For some reason, Collins's songs made me feel there was a life beyond selling drugs, and that I would be at peace one day.

Peter Gabriel's album *Us* contained some of the best music I ever heard. It took me to the level where I belonged. It was spiritual. I still vibe with this cat's music. He made one of the greatest songs of all times, a masterpiece called "Sky Blue."

My love for music led me to attend several concerts: Stephanie Mills, Cameo, Morris Day and the Time, Blue Magic, Keith Sweat, Frankie Beverly and Maze, and Phil Collins, to name a few. These concerts were my only true vacations.

One concert that really stood out was Phil Collins at Madison Square Garden. He ended the concert with a song called "Take Me Home." I connected with the song; it made me feel like I was on the wrong path in life. As I listened, I felt like I was lost and needed to get back home. To me, that's what music is really about. It should take you to places mentally and spiritually. The best music keeps you on level.

I sometimes think about my former lifestyle and reminisce about all the cars and money I left behind. When it came to these things, nobody in the streets could touch me, Rich, or Alpo. Anything street hustlers and rappers do today, we did at a younger age and at a much higher level.

Despite all our wealth and fame, I can honestly say that *we were the dumbest motherfuckers in America*! Each of us owned more than thirty cars; each car cost more than $50,000 apiece once we customized them. I estimate that we spent more than $4,500,000 on cars alone!

Lifestyles of the Rich and Infamous

Some Harlem residents may remember that brownstone townhouses sold for one dollar in the 1980s if you promised the city of New York you would renovate the building. With all the money we blew on cars, we could have owned several valuable properties in Harlem right now. Instead, we took our blood money and wasted it on foolish things.

I chose to sell all my property when I left the drug game in 1987. Rich can't enjoy his cars in his grave, and Alpo can't enjoy his cars in jail. This is why I say we were ignorant. We were rich, but never spent our wealth on things that made money in the future. All the older people around us knew better, but some failed to advise us. If they had, we probably wouldn't have listened anyway.

The Devil's Advocates

In truth, fiends aren't the only ones addicted to drugs. Dealers are addicted to selling them for the money it makes. As it turned out, hustlers weren't the only ones intoxicated by drug money. Cocaine made so much money that even people with legitimate jobs—including cats in law enforcement—got in on the action.

In a scene from *The Godfather*, Marlon Brando's character, Don Corleone, called a sit-down with the heads of all his rival Mafia families. Corleone, the boss of all bosses, was totally against drug trafficking.

The head of another family stood up in defense of selling drugs, arguing that it made enormous profit. He explained how $3,000 could turn into $100,000 in the drug trade. He went on to say they could keep the drugs away from schools and their residential areas. "Give it to the dark people," he said. "They're animals anyway. Let them lose their souls."

Game Over

Even a veteran criminal like the Godfather saw the damage drugs would cause, and voted against getting involved in the game. He refused to give the other dons access to his political connections for such a move. In real life, not only members of organized crime, but cops, lawyers, doctors, and other "legitimate" people got down with the drug game.

Malcolm X once noted that drugs, prostitution, gambling, and other forms of organized crime *could not exist without the cooperation and permission of law enforcement officials*, i.e., "the government." My experiences in the drug game bear witness to this statement.

Drugs come into this country through international drug cartels and the various government agents and military officials that sold out to these drug organizations. But when we read news reports or view documentaries about the narcotics industry, our long finger of blame points at the average low-level street corner dealer.

I am not saying that street dealers should go unpunished. I'm saying that dealers cannot take all the blame. We need to stop the bullshit and tell the truth. In the 1980s, all types of people were involved in the drug game.

I'll be the first to say that as a drug dealer, I helped to put poison in the community. In doing so, I was basically doing the devil's work. But as I mentioned before, I had major help. All the people who help drug dealers do their dirt are the devil's advocates. Corrupt cops were some of the major advocates.

The Sugar Hill section of Harlem where I grew up was

"protected and served" by the 30th Police Precinct, located on West 151st Street between Amsterdam and Convent Avenues. Their reputation for corruption earned them the nickname Dirty Thirty. According to a *New York Times* special report, "Perjury Dividend," published on January 5, 1997, the precinct's nickname was well deserved.

According to the article, officers routinely gave false testimony in more than 2,000 cases, stole money from local drug dealers, and even forced people to sell drugs. Some officers stole or copied drug dealers' apartment keys, then broke into their apartments and stole drugs, guns, and money.

In one case, officers from the precinct were secretly videotaped breaking into a local drug dealer's apartment and assaulting him to get drugs and money. In another case, officers stole a safe from a drug dealer's home, and then brought it to the precinct, where they got it open and took thousands of dollars.

Of course, Harlem's Dirty Thirty was not the only corrupt precinct in New York City. Black and Latino ghetto residents know that corrupt cops exist all over New York City and in fact, all over the country. When cocaine and crack invaded New York in the eighties, cops saw the boatloads of money brought in from drug busts. Just like street hustlers, some cops could not resist the temptation to make easy money by stealing from dealers or in extreme cases, having them sell drugs.

The last statement might sound harsh to individuals who believe all cops are fair and honest. Some people find it difficult to believe that some cops sell drugs. The cure for that is a little research into the Larry Davis story. Troy Reed's documentary, *The Larry Davis Story*, provides excellent information on this topic.

Larry Davis was a young black man living in the Bronx. The precinct in Davis's neighborhood was notoriously corrupt; cops routinely extorted dealers for money, stole money and drugs recovered in drug busts, and forced hustlers to sell drugs for them.

According to Reed's documentary, Larry Davis was one of several young men in the Bronx who sold drugs for corrupt cops during the 1980s. He stopped cooperating when he discovered why his pregnant girlfriend lost their baby: It was addicted to cocaine. Davis soon found out a cop regularly supplied his girlfriend with cocaine. Adding insult to injury, the cop who supplied the cocaine was also one of the cops Davis worked for.

Feeling betrayed by the cop and sad at the news of his child's death, Davis ended his business relationship with the rogue officers. This concerned the cops for two reasons. First, they did not want to stop making all the easy money that came from selling crack. Second, they feared Larry Davis might seek revenge by reporting their illegal activities. Furthermore, Davis allegedly owed the cops $40,000 in drug sales that he did not pay.

The cops wanted their money and they wanted to prevent Davis from snitching on them. So they falsely charged him with murdering four local drug dealers. This false charge gave them the reason they needed to eliminate Larry Davis.

On the night of November 19, 1986, six police officers

rushed the home of Davis's sister Gina, hoping to find Larry. Despite the presence of his mother, sister, nieces, and nephews, the officers began firing at Davis. They didn't come to arrest him, but to kill him. Davis owned several weapons himself, and somehow he shot all six officers and escaped into the night.

Police conducted one of the largest manhunts in New York State history. About seventeen days later, Davis turned himself over to the authorities, after first contacting the media and the FBI to protect himself from angry police officers.

Of course, the Larry Davis incident does not reflect on all police officers. There are cops throughout America who do their jobs honestly and do them well. However, the Larry Davis story confirms that police corruption and abuse still existed in American cities throughout the eighties. In fact, it continues today. The truth must be brought to light.

In Miami, Florida, during the mid-1980s, three men were killed and thrown into the ocean; this was the result of a $27 million cocaine deal gone bad. Apparently, a crooked cop was involved with the rip-off. I saw this story on *The FBI Files*.

The show explained how Cuban leader Fidel Castro released thousands of Cubans into Miami in the early eighties. According to the show, at least 15 percent of the people released were criminals. Many of these criminals came to America and got involved with cocaine trafficking.

Miami cops—drooling over all the money slipping by them—began stealing from cocaine dealers and killing them to eliminate witnesses. These dirty cops started buying expensive cars and houses with cash. One cop had $260,000 in a safe-deposit box. The FBI arrested six Miami police officers in 1986, but the judge declared a mistrial and the cops were released. The FBI was determined to put these cops away; failure to do so, they argued, would cause Miami residents to distrust cops.

Eventually federal agents got the evidence they needed when they convinced an officer to testify against his partners in exchange for a reduced sentence. A subsequent investigation identified seventeen cops involved in drug running and exhortation. One cop jumped bail and fled the country in a private jet. When the feds finally caught up with him he bribed them with offers of over $500,000 if they would let him go.

Further investigations discovered over a hundred cases of cops robbing and killing hustlers in Miami. Shows like *The FBI Files* reveal how serious this drug game really is. In fact, *The FBI Files* aired an episode called "The C-11 Squad" that focused on the deaths of Rich and Donnell Porter.

Unlike many people, my knowledge of corrupt cops did not come from a special news report, but from firsthand experience. I knew a few dirty cops in the 30th Precinct throughout my hustling years. The ones I knew informed me when to expect raids on my drug spots.

If I knew a certain spot was about to be raided by cops, I closed the spot down, let things cool off, then reopened the spot a few days later. After receiving information, I usually dropped maybe $500 or $1,000 cash on the ground or in a trash can where the cop could see it. I was never stupid enough to discuss payments with cops or directly hand money to them. One hand washed another.

Paying dirty cops was just another expense that a drug dealer had to deal with. This information kept my drug operations afloat. What usually hurt a hustler most was when a crooked cop stole money; this resulted in a business loss or expense the hustler didn't anticipate.

My first experience with the Dirty Thirty occurred in the lobby of my building. My older brother Kev and I were in the hallway. My brother had a gun and some drugs on him, and I held about $10,000 in cash.

Two black cops rolled up out of nowhere and pretty much had us busted. They searched us and quickly found we were dirty. We just knew we were going to jail. Imagine how surprised we were when they took about half of the money and the gun. *They allowed us to keep the drugs* and told us in that serious cop tone to "stay the fuck out of the building," or they'd take us downtown next time.

One time, I was riding with this Spanish cat who worked for Lulu. He could not understand or speak one word of English. Actually, he could say two words: "video store." Lulu owned a video store in the Washington Heights area of Manhattan. Lulu instructed him to say the words "video store" if cops stopped him and asked any questions.

Luck was not with us that day. The cops pulled us over by 159th Street and Broadway and told us to step outside the car. Luckily, we had no drugs on us, but we did have a bag in the trunk with about $50,000 cash. After a quick search, the cops found the bag and demanded to know where we got the money from and what we planned to do with it.

My Spanish associate repeatedly answered the cops by saying "Video store, video store." The cops became frustrated with his responses, and I feared the worst.

They asked him again: "Where did you get this money?"

Again he replied, "Video store."

The other cop asked him what his name was, and again he said, "Video store."

Meanwhile, I was thinking, "This fuckin' jackass!"

As I was thinking that we were going to spend the rest of this night in prison, one cop decided to grab several handfuls of cash and said to me, "Tell your friend, your buddy, this money we're taking is for the *video store!*" They kindly jumped back in their patrol car and left.

The longer I hustled, the more I began to feel like the NYPD's personal automated teller machine. It got to the point where cops would slowly cruise by in their cars, hoping to find me at one of my drug spots so they could get some money from me. Cops sometimes extorted money in very unusual ways.

For instance, I was in a sneaker store on 125th Street one day. An off-duty cop I knew saw me, did a double take, and then came into the store. I thought he was going to fuck with me, and search me for coke. Instead, he whispered in my ear, "Hey Azie. You know, me and my son like to buy sneakers too." I got the hint. I left $500 with the girl at the cash register whom I knew, and told her it was for the guy I was talking to. I told him he had a $500 credit and took off.

Some cops in the 'hood were jealous of young cats making so much money. Cops had to put in long hours in dangerous neighborhoods for little pay. While they drove beat-up, broken-down Fords and Toyotas, we sported BMWs, Saabs, and Mercedes. They likely figured, "We'll never stop them from selling drugs, but we can at least take some of their shit and live better ourselves."

On the other hand, many cops actually liked our style and gave us props, or respect. A few times, cops almost broke their necks trying to catch a glimpse of my ride. One time I was cruising through the 'hood in my brand-new Mercedes-Benz AMG Hammer 300CE coupe. The shit was ice-blue with butter-soft leather interior and no-body around the way had seen anything like it. The police drove by me then pulled a quick U-turn.

Asking me to get out, the officer got in my car and just drove the fuck off! I just stood there thinking, "What the fuck is this?" His partner just stood by the patrol car with that "Don't try anything stupid" look. Returning a few minutes later, the cop got out with a huge smile of sat-isfaction on his face; it resembled the look brothers have when they've just had some good sex.

"Listen, you haven't done anything wrong, buddy," he said. "I just had to drive that fucking car of yours."

I got back in my car and winked at the cops as I pulled off, watching them watch me.

My most memorable experience with a crooked cop in-volved a pretty black female cop. She and her girlfriend pulled up to a light by a stoop where I was chillin'. They were riding in a burgundy Volkswagen Jetta. They kept looking in my direction and pointing, so I assumed they wanted to buy some coke. Since I never saw them before, I didn't say anything; they would have to approach me first.

The sister on the passenger side smiled and motioned me to come over. I did the same. She motioned again. Finally I decided to go check her out. She had that look in her eyes. We played the small-talk game for a few minutes and eventually she told me she was a cop working in Spanish Harlem. She also told me she knew who I was. We exchanged phone numbers and she made me promise to call her.

We started to chill together. I witnessed the benefits of being a police officer. She gave me this special police sticker to put on the back of my car. I put it on a small black Peugeot I had at the time. My boy Whip and I were driving one day with a brick of cocaine in the trunk. When we heard the cops ask us to pull over, our hearts stopped; getting busted with a kilo of cocaine could have cost us a lifetime in prison.

I quickly said to Whip, "If they ask us to get out the car, you take off running, and I'll pull off. You go one way and I'll go the other way. I'm not going to jail."

Whip replied, "Say no more."

The cops approached on both sides of the car, with their flashlights probing for something illegal.

One cop said, "I noticed your police sticker. Are you an officer?"

"No," I replied. "My sister is."

Thanks to that sticker, we didn't have to go on a wild police chase. Who knows what the outcome would have been.

One night the sexy police officer and I went on a double date with her girlfriend and my boy Lou. She weaved in and out of traffic on the highway; she was doing at least ninety to one hundred miles per hour. I told her to chill and slow down before cops pulled us over. She looked at me, smirked, and continued speeding. The cops did pull us over. Nevertheless, after she flashed her badge, the cop smiled and said, "What's the hurry? Is everything okay?"

She replied, "Everything is good, Officer."

The cop said, "Excuse me, my bad. Have a nice day, Officer."

After eating at a very expensive restaurant, we got a hotel room and she really showed her wild side. She stripped naked and danced around the room. My "gun" was ready to aim and fire! Then she emptied the bullets from her gun. She wanted me to place the gun to her head and "force" her to suck my dick! I was suspicious but eventually my morality won out. How could I resist an officer of the law?

We had a number of crazy adventures with each other and we became close. I felt comfortable around her, which was weird since she was a cop and I was a dealer. This comfortable feeling led me to develop a little bit of trust in her, which turned out to be a mistake.

After explaining that I wanted to purchase a new Jeep

Cherokee, she came up with a plan that would supposedly help both of us. "I'm selling my car," she said. "Why don't you take it and trade it in for the vehicle you want? Then whatever the difference is between the two vehicles you give me in cash."

I agreed with the plan. The car dealer informed me that since the trade-in car was in a different name, I would have to register the new vehicle in that same person's name. I did that, and everything seemed fine. I left with a brand-new Jeep, and gave her the cash.

After a few weeks rolled by, she started calling me all the time, asking me to stop parking the car around my various drug spots. She was afraid that police would run my license plate and all her information would come up.

I told her to take the Jeep for a few days, drive it around, and maybe that would help her relax. She came and got the Jeep, and I never heard from her again. I called her once, and she responded like a police officer rather than a friend. "Don't ever call this number again," as if we never met. Ain't that a bitch!

Cops receive a lot of heat for being corrupt, but they are not the only ones. I sold drugs to lawyers, doctors, paramedics, pro basketball players, actors, Grammy Award–winning singers, Wall Street brokers, you name it. You wouldn't believe the names of people I sold drugs to. This was the *Scarface*, Pablo Escobar, Noriega, and Oliver North era. The question wasn't "who used cocaine during this time?" The question was "who *wasn't* using it?"

There was lots of money involved, and a majority of people took payola. My goal is not to point fingers or expose anyone. I just want the judgment to be fair. Society puts the blame on petty dealers and users, but the problem is much larger than that.

"Let he who is without sin throw the first stone." The petty hustler does the dirty work for people in high places, and catch all the heat or jail time. However, low-level dealers simply could not operate without help from so-called legitimate sources.

My experiences with corrupt individuals, especially cops, taught me a lot about how this society deals with black people. Cops have the power, money, and training to stop just about whatever crime they want to stop. I found that police permit some forms of crime and condemn others.

While waiting for a train one day, I noticed two teenagers sneak in without paying. Two young-looking cats, dressed casually, quickly confronted them. No one would have guessed they were police officers. If the cops dressed in full uniform, the teenagers would not have attempted to hop the train. This made me wonder, "Are the cops trying to prevent crime, or do they want to simply catch people committing crime?" Instead of using sneaky methods to catch these kids, the cops should have prevented the crime in the first place.

If uniformed police officers patrolled city blocks, had a visible presence on the streets, and were courteous to citizens, things would change for the better in the communities they patrol. Their very presence alone would cause crime to drop, because it would deter people from doing something that would get them into trouble. *Cops are not stupid. They may not have all the answers, but they do have some knowledge of what causes, prevents, and ends crime. If they are not doing the things necessary to prevent or stop crime, perhaps they actually want certain crimes in certain neighborhoods to occur.*

I can personally say that from 1984 to 1993 police corruption, crime, and violence were widespread in New York City, and especially in Harlem. This period of chaos and corruption was part of what I believe was a plan to control people of color in America's ghettos. Many major trends begin in Harlem, and then spread to other boroughs and across the country. Harlem is the head of the American inner city, and once you kill the head, you destroy the body.

Heroin was the drug of choice in Harlem in the 1970s. In the eighties, cocaine appeared in Harlem, then its more addictive and less expensive cousin, crack, took over. With the appearance of cocaine, Harlem suffered from a flood of drug-related crime and violence. In fact, it seemed as if people could run wild, do whatever they wanted to do, and get away with it.

Long single-file lines of people would sometimes stretch down an entire block. These cheese lines, as we called them, represented countless people waiting to purchase cocaine or crack. You also saw actual cheese lines of people waiting to receive free blocks of cheese or other food from the government.

The difference was that drug cheese lines formed all over Harlem, day and night. Police would walk or drive right past these lines without investigating. They knew what was happening because they kept a close eye on blocks known for heavy drug traffic. In other words, they allowed dealers to sell cocaine and crack.

In the nineties, New York City anti-drug campaigns became strict. TNT (Tactical Narcotics Teams) units formed in police precincts and gave cops larger weapons and budgets to combat drugs. Police arrested tons of drug dealers while the courts smacked them with excessive sentences. Police departments recruited more black and Latino officers to help them catch black and Latino drug dealers and users.

Toy stores and police precincts teamed up to encourage citizens to turn guns in to their local precinct. In exchange, they received a small sum of money or a gift certificate to purchase toys for their children. Supposedly, individuals could turn in a gun with "bodies" (murders) on it and the cops would not run a check on the gun or the person presenting it.

By now, the government plan was complete. One part of the black community was addicted to drugs. Another part of the community wasted away in America's prisons and correctional facilities. Another section of the black population was murdered by cops and street rivals in the drug war.

The remaining blacks were largely unemployed, uneducated, and disarmed. Strict laws and brutal police made Harlem "safe again." In 1970, the United States Congress passed the Racketeer Influenced and Corrupt Organizations Act, known as the RICO Act. The law was originally used to destroy the Mafia, but was later applied to drug organizations during the eighties and nineties. The RICO Act was used to throw thousands of people into jail.

From the late nineties until now, Harlem witnessed several urban renewal programs. Outside contractors rebuilt tenement buildings and brownstones, while local politicians struck deals to bring popular chain stores uptown.

Harlem property values soared and now, it is okay to live in Harlem again. Whites moved back into Harlem, buying up its most valuable and beautiful property. New black businesses appeared, but most blacks and Latinos continued to suffer from slum living conditions.

The corruption I experienced in Harlem during the eighties and nineties was described by Malcolm X as a trap. The law catches you when it chooses to. It *allows* certain crimes and criminals to exist to make money off them. The growth of the prison industry is a good example.

After the Civil War, black people gained political power and education for the first time in America. Prejudiced whites did not like seeing their former slaves become powerful.

Therefore, they came up with a plan. Racist groups like the Ku Klux Klan formed, using mob violence to destroy black homes, churches, and leadership. They used force to prevent the freedmen from voting or holding political offices.

The lawmakers helped by creating the Thirteenth Amendment to the Constitution. We're taught in school that this amendment ended slavery in the United States, which is partially true. However, a closer reading of the amendment shows us something different:

"Neither slavery nor involuntary servitude, except as a punishment for crime whereof the party shall have been duly convicted, shall exist within the United States . . ."

Translation: It is illegal to enslave a person or force them do work against their will with little or no pay *unless they have been convicted of a crime!* They ended slavery but then created it in another form. This means that once you enter the prison system, you become a virtual slave of the state. This is why they replace your name with a number, don't allow you to wear the clothes you want, keep you in metal cages like animals, and tell you when to eat, sleep, wake up, and go outside.

Most important, states make money from inmates who build computers, do construction, and create furniture for wages comparable to what sweatshop workers make in foreign countries. To make matters worse, private citizens own shares of stock in some of these prisons. In other words, they want to see more prisons built and filled to capacity. Mass incarceration is simply another hustle by the government. The more prisons they fill, the more cheap labor the society has. Notice what people make up the majority of America's prisons: poor, uneducated blacks and Latinos.

When it comes to corruption, devil's advocates exist in all colors, come from all economic backgrounds, and have various religious beliefs. The true battle is not racial but spiritual. It is not about black and white, but wrong or right. If people truly want to resolve the drug problem in this country, they have to clean house and expose all the people who make the drug game work.

I believe the universe is governed by divine or "cosmic" laws. Those who fail to live in accordance with those laws will ultimately pay the price for their actions. In my former world of hustling, those directly involved with the game suffered, those indirectly involved with the game suffered, and some who were innocent but related to those in the game suffered. I did not know it at the time, but my own involvement in the game would result in tragedies I did not foresee.

10
Game Over

August 20, 1987, was a day I'll never forget. I recall playing ball in the park on 128th Street and Lexington Avenue. Kev, my man Charlie Cee, and I played Dapper Dan, Wayne, and Gums for five gees, or $5,000. We lost the first game; it was real close. Then we ran it back. My man Charlie was real hype in the second game. He talked shit the entire time.

"Fuck that, A. These niggas trying to play us; they think they got something sweet here! Let's play. You stay down low and bang with that nigga; he can't stop you, baby! I got my man all day. He's a bum, yo! Kev, take him to the basket, he can't stop you."

We went to work. I never saw Charlie act like that before, but he put the fire in us. We blew the other team out. They wanted to run it back, but Charlie walked out the park upset.

"Nah, we not fucking with y'all cheating motherfuckers." We were sweating bullets. We walked back to the block, and I told my man Lou to drive the car; I didn't want to fuck up the leather and mess up that new car smell, you know?

As we walked back to the block, a large crowd of people, about a hundred, followed us back to the location on 132nd Street.

When we reached the block, my man Sherman walked up to us and said, "We *been* done and there's mad heads out around the spot looking to cop."

I went to the phone to call my aunt Joann Blue to see if she was home (I had to go to her house to get the coke), but no one picked up. It was a very hot August night so I thought she was hanging out at Bonita's, a bar on 139th Street and Lenox Avenue. As I hung up the phone, she pulled right up on me in her car. She was obviously tipsy and there were two passengers in her car.

"You looking for me, Azie?"

"Yeah," I told her.

"I'm going home right now—give me a minute," she said.

"Okay, then I'll be right behind you," I replied.

I went to the corner store, bought some water, and then sat down on the stoop. Charlie came and sat next to me. He wanted some work.

"Yo, A, let me rock tonight; I need some extra paper!"

"No problem," I said. "Yo, Charlie . . . what got into you on the court?"

"A, I'm tired of niggas trying to play us and besides that, I play better when I talk shit."

"I feel you," I said. "I am tired of all this bullshit too—money, cars, hoes, selling drugs—how long we gonna be doing this shit? For the rest of our lives?"

"You right, man. We gotta change, think bigger than this."

At that point, a girl named Lynette Bell walked up on me. I'd been trying to get with her for a while.

"I was looking for you all day. Where were you?" she asked. I tried to keep my distance because I was wet and sweaty from balling. On top of that, it felt like it was over a hundred degrees outside. The Lord was in full effect. I was, like, "Why are you looking for me? You always stand me up."

She responded by whispering something sexy in my ear. She finally gave me the green light to get with her.

"Okay," I said "But I got to make a run real quick . . . I'll be right back." I was lusting for sure.

"No," Lynette replied, "I'm not waiting, I been waiting all day for you. Why can't I come with you? I'm ready right now!"

I looked right into her eyes and said, "Fuck it, come on and ride with us." I usually didn't let women come with me on a business run, but if you saw her you would think twice too.

We jumped in a cab and headed up to 169th Street and the Grand Concourse in the Bronx, to my aunt's apartment building. During the entire cab ride, Lynette kept saying she had to use the bathroom. I paid it no mind at the time.

When we reached my aunt's building I saw that Joanne's

car was double parked right in front. "Good, they're here," I thought. I called up to the window, "Joanne, Joanne." Nobody came to the window. I was thinking, "I know she's up there. Her car is parked right here." So I shouted her name again—still no answer. All of a sudden, the keys flew out the window. This was strange; usually she would look out the window and drop the keys down when she recognized me.

"Something isn't right. Let me go to the pay phone and call upstairs," I thought. I quickly looked around for police, just in case they rolled on the crib.

My man Charlie was persistent: "Come on, A, mad heads are waiting on the block. Let's go get this money. Stop being so paranoid. Besides, your homegirl over there has to use the bathroom." Lynette quickly agreed. "I have to use the bathroom *real* bad." I hesitated for a second, and then told them to come with me. I usually followed my first instinct. But Charlie and Lynette pressured me, so I gave in.

Joanne wasn't really my aunt, just a very good friend. She would do anything that I asked, and the feeling was mutual. She put apartments and cars for me in her name. I saw her as family, so it was only right to call her Auntie.

We climbed the stairs to my aunt's house and knocked on the door. The door flew open. Someone holding an Uzi and wearing a stocking cap over their head grabbed me, pulled me into the apartment, and pushed me to the floor. Two other cats came off the staircase and pulled Charlie and Lynette into the apartment.

I looked up at this creep, who kept saying, "You did

me wrong. You did me wrong." I said, "Kevin Clark, that's you?" after I caught his voice. "Kev, what the fuck are you doing?"

"What does it look like, motherfucker? Don't say my name again or you're a dead man!"

One of his men pulled my safe from the bedroom into the living room where I was lying on the floor. Kevin told him to take Charlie and Lynette in the bedroom with the others. Kevin started yelling at me again.

"Open the safe! Open the safe before I kill you!"

"Yo, Kev, why are you doing this?" I said.

He hit me with his gun real hard right above my eye. Blood covered my whole face.

"I told you not to say my name again. Now open the safe, motherfucka, before I kill you!"

I tried my best to open the safe but I couldn't. I was nervous as hell. Blood poured into my eyes and I couldn't see. I couldn't believe Kevin would do this. We were cool, or so I thought.

Kevin Clark used to date my sister back in the day. At that time, he worked in a grocery store on 134th Street and Seventh Avenue. An old-timer named Mr. Vincent used to sell coke in the back of the store. To make a long story short, Mr. Vincent was found dead in his apartment, cut to pieces and stuffed in an old trunk. Kevin started freebasing real bad at the time. A crack addict will do anything to get their paws on some crack.

After Mr. Vincent's death, Kevin went into hiding. Word on the street was that someone put a contract on his head. As a result, Kev laid low in a downtown hotel.

Game Over

One day my sister told me he wanted to speak with me. I was not in the game at this time; I was just a kid. I was trying to figure out what the hell he wanted with me. My sister gave me the address to the hotel and convinced me to go to see him.

I went downtown to the Skyline hotel on Forty-ninth Street and Tenth Avenue to meet him. I knocked on the door and that motherfucka swung the door open real fast. While pointing a gun to my face, he pulled me inside and pushed me against the wall to frisk me.

"Yo, anybody can take this contract. I can't trust nobody. No disrespect. You understand where I'm coming from."

Actually I didn't understand. I was scared and thinking, "What the hell is he doing this for?" He was cracked up out of his mind and he looked like a monster. His eyes were big as fifty-cent pieces, and red like fire.

"Yo, Azie, I need you to do me a big favor. I need you to give this to your man Rich. Tell him to move this for me."

With that, he handed me a bag full of coke, about half a kilo. I didn't want to do shit for Kevin, but I saw him standing there coked up with a loaded gun. I decided to be smart.

"Yeah, whatever you say," I replied.

He warned me not to cross him as he pointed the gun to my head. "Do this for me, man. Call me. Don't let me down. I need your help."

"All right, Kev, I got you," I said nervously.

When he let me out I thanked God and got on the uptown train. "What the fuck did my sister get me into?" I kept thinking to myself. I went home, gave her the drugs, and told her to give it back to Kevin.

"I'm not with this. Fuck him. He's crazy and you're crazy for fuckin' with that nut. He's going get you killed. He's a crackhead."

She eventually did give the coke back to Kevin. Just days later, while riding the A train, Kevin fell asleep with two guns on him. A couple of quick-thinking Guardian Angels—a New York City vigilante group that patrolled the subways—held Kevin until the police arrived. He was found guilty of gun and drug possession and wound up doing six years in prison. He wasn't released from prison until February 1987.

Those years went by quickly and a lot changed. I wasn't a kid anymore. I'd moved up to the major leagues on the street, and I was in charge. Kevin heard stories about me while he served time, but probably couldn't believe it. Once he got out, he saw it for himself: Rich, AZ, and Alpo had Harlem on lock!

When they released Kevin from prison, I looked out for him. I gave him a car—my drop-top Saab—I gave him a block that moved about a brick a week, and I took him shopping. I put $15,000 in his pocket. All he had to do was fall back, relax, and count his money. What more can you expect when you're on parole? He was a hot target for cops and I didn't want the heat on him to bring me down.

Now there I was, looking at a man I had taken care of trying to rob me. I couldn't believe the motherfucker— standing over me like a madman, talking shit about how I did him wrong. He was cracked out of his mind. Thoughts ran through my head. What goes around comes back around. Cocaine was a powerful form of negative energy that I helped put into the community. What I sent out had just returned to sender. This was my judgment day.

Kevin got angrier because I couldn't open the safe. Come on, let's be real. The blood in my eyes blinded me. He snatched the stocking cap off his head and told me to open the safe. I looked—through the blood pouring down my face—right into his eyes. He looked crazy like he did that night at the hotel.

I had to think quickly. I started talking real fast, trying to come up with a plan to hopefully save us from being killed.

"Listen, man, there's no money in the safe. I got $150,000 at my crib in Jersey. Take me to the house . . . I'll give it to you. Just don't hurt nobody."

His eyes lit up at the thought of the money. "A hundred fifty? Don't play me like you did before. You did me wrong," he insisted.

"Yo, Kev, I didn't play you."

"Yes you did! Now get the fuck up. You can't leave like this. You got blood all over you."

"I got blood all over myself," I repeated in my mind. *This motherfucker is crazy!* He pulled me up, then kicked me in the back toward the bathroom.

"Wash your face. You got something to wear here?" I told him I didn't, and then his man came into the bathroom. Kev told his partner about the plan to take me to New Jersey so they could get the cash.

The whole idea about going to Jersey was really my

plan to get outside so we could make a run for it. I was ready to take the chance of getting shot in the back. Then again, maybe they wouldn't shoot because it would draw attention. I figured that making a run outside was better than getting shot in the house; it might also save everybody's life. It was worth a try.

One of Kevin's partners took off his shirt and handed it to me. He told me to put it on because I was going with them. I thought they were going for my plan. "We might get out alive," I thought. That's when Joanne panicked and started to yell in the bedroom. "No, Junior," she said, using her nickname for me, "Don't go with them. Please, Junior, just give them what they want so that they can leave us alone." Then she turned her attention to the gunmen: "Just leave us alone . . . leave us alone!"

Kevin couldn't afford to have people making too much noise; neighbors might hear and call the police. He turned to one of his partners and told him to "shut that bitch up now!" The next thing I knew, someone turned the stereo up real loud. I stopped washing my face and just stared at Kevin, pointing his gun at me.

"What you looking at me like that for? You trying to play me again? I know there's some money in here," he said.

I knew all bets were off. They were going to kill my aunt and maybe all of us. I'd had enough.

"Kev, you a real sucker, a real bitch."

At that same moment, I heard the wicked gunshots go up in the air. I charged at Kevin and fought for my life. I almost had him until his man came out of the bedroom and placed his gun right on my forehead. I felt the coldness of the steel and braced myself as I watched him pull the trigger. *Boom!*

I didn't feel a thing.

All I heard was a loud noise. The sound echoed in my head as my spirit left my body and ascended into a peaceful bright light. I was in the presence of God, the most high. "God, please, I don't want to die," I prayed. Then my spirit slowly floated down back into my body.

I opened my eyes and found myself lying on the bathroom floor in a huge puddle of my own blood. There was so much blood that I started to slip and stumble. I had to hold on to the sink just to pull myself up.

I staggered into the bedroom to a sight I'll never forget; everyone lay motionless, each shot in the head and left for dead. "Oh, God no," I thought. I shook Charlie first. "Come on, man, get up. Please come back. They're gone, it's alright now." Then I turned to the others. "Joanne, Myra, please . . . Lynette, Michael . . ."

Nobody responded. I felt so bad, so guilty. It was my fault. I lay in the bed, pulled the covers over my bloody head, and tried my best to go to sleep. I wanted to die, just moments after I asked God to spare my life. I passed out in shock from losing so much blood.

I woke up on a stretcher in Lincoln Hospital. The Bronx district attorney and a homicide detective stood over me. My girl Pat stood on my left and my mother on my right. I heard Pat say, "You can't leave us, Azie. Think of your daughter Lorrell."

I thought back to the morning of the day I was shot. My daughter Lorrell cried so hard when I was about to leave the house. I had to double back and chill with her for about a half hour just to calm her down. I tried to tell her I had to take care of business and that I wouldn't be long. She wasn't having it. Children have a special sense.

I wish I'd listened to my three-year-old daughter. Maybe this would have never happened. Pat kept saying, "Just think of your daughter. What is she going to do without you?"

My mom was concerned with finding the person responsible for shooting me.

"Who did this to you, Junior? Who did this?" she asked, crying, out of her mind. I told her it was Kevin.

"Who?"

"Kevin, Ma. Kevin Clark, Pie's old boyfriend."

"Oh, God, no! Kevin killed my son!" I reminded her that I wasn't dead . . . yet.

The district attorney started talking to the doctor. He and the detective wanted to speak to me alone.

"Listen, we need five minutes alone with him," he said with authority. The doctor tried to tell them that I needed immediate medical attention, but his plea fell on deaf ears.

"We need five minutes alone with him, so we need everyone to leave the room now." My mother left, crying and yelling at the top of her lungs. Pat was obviously sad too. But I dealt with a lot of other chicks while I was seeing her, so I couldn't help but feel she thought I deserved this attack.

When everyone left the detective pulled out a tape recorder.

"I'm going to place this right here on your chest. We

want to ask you some questions. Are you conscious?" I nodded my head.

"Can you speak?" I told them I could. With that, they got right to the point.

"Look, you know you're dying, right?" Shocked, I said no.

"The doctors say there is no chance that you will recover. You know that, right?"

"Now I do," I said, even more shocked.

"Everybody else who was in the apartment with you is dead. You're the only one left that we can talk to. We want to catch the people responsible for this massacre. Are you conscious?"

"I'm okay," I responded. News that all those people died had me in a daze.

"We're going to ask you some questions to make sure you're conscious. Who is the president?"

"Reagan, I think."

"What am I holding in my right hand?"

"A pen."

"Okay, good. What is that on your chest?"

"A tape recorder."

"That's right. Now tell us who shot you at 1295 Grand Concourse, apartment 3B, tonight."

"Kevin Clark," I mumbled.

"Did you say Kevin Clark?"

"Yes."

"Did he act alone?"

"No, there were two others."

"Did you say two others?"

"Yes."

"Were they black or Spanish?"

"Black."

"Do you know their names?"

"No, I never saw them before."

"Do you know what kind of gun Kevin used?"

"It looked like an Uzi."

"How about the other two, what kind of guns did they have?"

"I'm not sure. It looked like a . . ." I began to feel weak, and I started to fade away.

The detective and the D.A. were impatient. Believing I would die any minute, they wanted to get as much information from me as they could.

"Come on, hang with us, Azie. Tell me, were drugs involved?"

"No drugs," I mumbled before I passed out.

I woke up after my operation the next day. The first thing that came into focus was my room number, 126. I couldn't move, which made me think I was paralyzed. I began to feel sorry for myself. Images of all the people who had died filled my head. Why me? I thought. I looked out for everyone, even Kevin. I put him on and made sure he was straight, or so I thought. I even threw money up in the air and gave money to the homeless. I took care of my entire family. "I am a giver, not a taker," I thought. "Why me, Father? Why?"

In my deepest thoughts I heard this peaceful voice: *"What you gave is not of me."*

Just then, I started to move my legs. I could still walk! I

thanked God immediately. The doctor walked in the room to check on my progress.

"Good morning, Azie. How do you feel?"

"I can't move everything, but I can move my legs."

"You'll be okay. The anesthesia has to wear off. You'll be fine. It's good to see that you're up and talking. You're very lucky to be alive. God must have some great plans for you. Hey, get some rest. I'll be back to check on you."

Police stood guard outside my room. Members of the press waited out front to interview me. The story made the headlines of the major New York City newspapers. The network television news channels aired the story too.

In order to visit me you had to go to the local precinct to get your picture taken and be fingerprinted. So you know I didn't have many visitors. Even members of my own family had to have a special pass to visit. It was crazy. I kept thinking, "What the hell have I gotten myself into?"

My man Lulu was the first non–family member to visit me. He went through all those procedures. I'll never know how he managed not to get caught. I remember he entered my room upset and in tears.

"No, Azito, no, Azito, look at you! Your head . . . who could want to do this to you?"

"I did it to myself, Lulu, I did it to myself."

"No way, no good. I'll take care of this fuckin' motherfucker."

"Lulu, no. *Mucho* police involved, just forget about it."

"I can't stay, Azito. I can't stay any longer. I can't see you like this. Your head . . . this hurts. Didn't I tell you to stay low? Didn't I tell you? But you no listen. You go buy all those cars, putting all the evil eyes on you. Look at you now!"

He walked out, upset and cursing heavily. "Fuck that! This fuckin' motherfucker is dead! I'll find him. I know you don't tell me. But they tell me Kevin."

His tears and concern were sincere. I felt his love. The police rushed in the room, and asked if I was okay. I told them I was.

"What's wrong with that guy?" one officer asked, referring to Lulu.

"He's okay, officer. He's just upset."

Neither Rich nor Alpo paid me a visit. Stan came through with a message from them saying they were looking all over for Kevin.

"Yo, Stan, tell Rich and 'Po to fall back. God got this. The police know everything."

"Somebody got to pay for this, Azie."

"Did you hear me, man? Leave it alone."

"I'm sorry, A, somebody got to die," Stan said, still resisting my call for peace.

"You don't get it, Stan. Somebody *did* pay. Somebody *did* die: Charlie, Joanne . . . everybody in that apartment with me. Can't you see?"

Stan started to cry. He asked me if I was okay. He probably thought I had lost my mind. The truth was that I *found* my mind. I asked him to leave because he was stressing me out. Stan walked out, shaking his head as if I was crazy.

The cops were right outside my door. For all I knew,

they could've had the room bugged. It seemed like nobody was thinking. Everybody acted crazy.

Hours after Stan left, my mother and Pat came to see me again. They informed me that Charlie, Joanne, and Myra had died. Lynette lived, along with Michael Lamar. "That's great," I thought. "God gave them a second chance." I was relieved that some people lived, but still felt guilty for those who didn't.

"I am so sorry, Pat. Forgive me."

"Please don't worry about that," she said. "Pull yourself together and get better. Your health is more important than anything right now. You need all your strength. Everybody's praying for you to get better."

I asked about my daughter Lorrell. I was surprised Pat didn't bring her to see me.

"I didn't want to bring her," Pat explained. "I don't want her to see you like this."

My mother told me that Kevin turned himself in to the Virginia police. Just then, two detectives walked in the room with more information.

"Hey, Azie, we got some good news. We got Kevin Clark in custody. He admits he was there but denies shooting anybody. We know that's a lie because we took three different kinds of bullets out of your body: a nine millimeter, one of these," he said, pointing to his gun, "a .38 special, and a .45 caliber. Yeah, you're a very lucky young man to be alive. You doctor said he didn't know how you survived . . . it's a miracle. By the way, Kevin Clark gave us the other two guys that helped him: Ronald Timmons and Henry Bolding."

Game Over

Ronald Timmons is already infamous; he's the reason they made the juvenile law where a teen can be tried as an adult. His buddy Henry Bolding is known for killing, and for robbing old ladies for their purses over there in Webster Projects. What a rap sheet! These guys are real fuckin' scumbags. They all did time together in the same prison upstate, and they all were released around the same time.

"Hey, Azie, the young girl that was with you at the apartment . . . was that your girlfriend?" the detective asked I told them she wasn't.

"So what was a thirteen-year-old kid doing with you?"

This information shocked me. She told me she was eighteen.

"Thirteen years old?" I asked to make sure I heard right.

"Yeah, thirteen. You didn't bang her, did you?"

"No," I replied. "But being honest, I was about to. She told me she was eighteen."

"How old are you, Azie?"

"Twenty-two."

"Well, you're lucky you didn't bang her, because we would be putting cuffs on you right now. Well, get better, get yourself some rest. You look much better than last night. By the way, nice cars you got there. We like that house in New Jersey too."

They wanted me to know they knew about my hustling.

"Tell Rich and Alpo to be careful with all those houses and cars. But don't worry about it. Luckily for you guys, narcotics is not our line of work. We're not here for that.

Game Over

We want to put away murderers. Kevin is talking to us. What else can he do? He's in a fucked-up predicament. Anyway, Azie, we will be back to talk to you soon. Take care of yourself."

"Damn, they know everything!" I thought.

My mother showed me the *New York Post* headline after the detectives left. It read: "Blood Bath in the Bronx: 5 Left for Dead."

Reporters were ready to storm the room. I asked Pat to call my lawyer Jack and tell him to handle the situation. I didn't want to talk to anyone. Pat got Jack on the phone. He spoke to some reporters and the next thing I knew, they were gone.

Visiting hours were over, so my mother and Pat left. My doctor came by and said the operation went well and everything looked good. He told me I would leave in a couple of days and that I was lucky to be alive. "The man upstairs must have better plans for you," he repeated. Those words hit me again. The Holy Spirit was present, and I felt so humble. I just wanted to be alone in silence, and I got my wish. Little did I know that my silence would be much louder than noise.

I began to hear and listen to God. I saw how God had spared my life so many times before. Things would have been different if I just listened to my first instinct. I realized how the decision to sell drugs put the lives of my loved ones in jeopardy.

When the creeps, crooks, suckas, and haters come, they come for everybody in your camp. They can't afford to leave witnesses. This is one game where you can't call "timeout." There is no referee in the game of death. This is a game where the rules change, bend, break, and sometimes don't exist.

My mind was spinning. So many thoughts flooded my brain. I thought back to my childhood when my family watched *The Ten Commandments* on television. My parents made us watch it every year. I was scared of that movie, especially the scene when Moses went up to Mount Sinai and began talking to God in the burning bush.

My room was located in the back of the apartment, and it was cold. I kept an electric heater burning throughout the winter. Once after watching that movie, I got really spooked at bedtime. I fell a sleep almost immediately but was awakened late in the night by a voice that seemed to come from my heater. "Azie . . . Azie . . . Azie."

It was just like the movie, but instead of a burning bush, God spoke to me from a portable heater. I jumped out of bed and sprinted down the hall into my mother and father's bedroom. My heart was pounding and I was visibly scared to death.

"What the hell is wrong with you, boy?" my mother asked.

"God's in my room," I responded, still shaking.

"God is in everybody's room," my father said in an attempt to calm me.

"No, Daddy, He's in my room *right now*, calling my name! Please can I sleep in here with you?"

Visions and recollections kept coming to me as I lay in that hospital bed. I remembered a dream in which my oldest sister had me climb a tall ladder. She pushed me toward the ceiling saying, "God wants you, God wants you." As I began to slowly penetrate the ceiling, I woke up in a cold sweat. It seemed like my whole life God was trying to get my attention.

Then I began to recall all the death that surrounded me in the past. I saw a building on St. Nicholas Avenue, near where I lived. There was a game room on the first floor, and I used to play Ms. Pac-Man there every day. The super of the building was cool.

One day while I was playing Ms. Pac-Man, the super came over and said, "Stay out of here. I'm about to kill everybody in this building. Nobody wants to pay me my money. You hear me, boy? Stay out of here."

Something about the way he said it and the look in his eyes told me he wasn't playing. I left the game room and went home. That night I heard gunshots. While heading to school the next morning, I noticed several paramedics and police officers out in front of that building. The super kept his word. He shot and killed five people in the building. Afterward, he went downtown to his parole officer and turned himself in.

I lay there in the hospital, having barely cheated death. Yet, my experience was not as unique as one might think. Murder and random acts of violence were typical in my neighborhood, and in my business. Now, death had hit home, along with thoughts of jail time. "This is serious, the police know everything. We're all going to prison," I thought. "Kevin told them everything." I began to analyze Kevin's motives for attacking me. Everybody in prison knows about events in the street. Prisoners often get the news about events on the outside just as it breaks. Kevin and his partners knew I was getting plenty of cash so they probably planned this heist in prison.

After Kevin revealed his accomplices, the police rounded them up and took the case to trial. I know Kevin and his accomplices didn't want me to show up. I didn't want to get involved with the courts either. Usually situations like that get handled on the street. But my lawyer convinced me to go or risk a full investigation on me. He told me he would arrange immunity so that nothing prior to the day of my attack would be held against me in court.

The day I testified, the district attorney asked the judge to grant me immunity and the judge agreed. The courtroom was filled with people, including my family and my attacker's family. There I was, looking at Kevin and his boys face-to-face. The tables turned. Now they sat before me fearing for their freedom.

Sitting in that courtroom forced me to put things in perspective. I thought about how things should have gone down. The same way my crew made all that loot in Harlem, Kevin and his boys could have done so also. We had the potential to make millions together with our combined strength. If he'd approached me as a businessman and not a street thug, he would have made millions of dollars over time. Because he chose the weak way out, he got only $5,000, a piece of jewelry, and a day in court.

This ordeal reminds me of that fairy tale about the

goose that laid the golden eggs. Some guy found a goose that laid solid gold eggs. Over time, the guy got rich from the goose eggs. But the man became greedy. He didn't want to wait for the goose to lay the golden eggs. So one day he sliced the goose wide open, thinking he would find dozens of golden eggs inside. Instead, he found no eggs and his greed had caused him to kill the source of his wealth! I was the goose, and Kevin Clark had tried to kill me to get a few gold eggs.

Instead of pulling the gun on me, Kevin should have wanted to jump in front of the gun for me. You always protect your bread and butter. My heart has never been filled with hatred. If I had died on that fateful night, and the coroner performed an autopsy on my body, they would have found a heart made of pure, solid gold love.

When the time came for me to answer the district attorney, I told the truth with no hesitation.

"Did you ever sell drugs, Mr. Faison?"

"Yes, I did."

"And what quantity of drugs did you sell?"

"That's not important," I replied, feeling insulted. As a tear rolled down my face, I continued: "No amount of drugs I sold gave them the right to gun us down like that in cold blood."

Kevin and his accomplices were pronounced guilty and each received 125 years in prison—basically a life sentence—for three murders and three attempted murders. Ronald Timmons turned and started yelling at Michael Lamar—whom he'd almost killed—after hearing his sentence. "I hope you drop dead and die from AIDS." He'd tried to take this man's life and actually got mad at him for getting locked up! He was out of his mind.

Henry Bolding, the other shooter, wasn't much better. His last words were "I hope the Yankees stay in the Bronx." I watched this on television, and it was sad to see. Kevin, the leader of the attack, just held his head down in shame throughout the entire trial.

11

Snitching

There was a no-snitching code on the street, yet I'd named Kevin Clark as my attacker. Rappers, drug dealers, and the media are talking about snitches these days.

Some people have suggested I'm a snitch for testifying against Kevin Clark, but the term is used so much these days that it has lost its meaning. To "snitch" means you go to the cops and squeal on somebody else (usually somebody on your team) to lessen your jail time; you get someone else in trouble to reduce the trouble you're in.

When I got shot in 1987, I didn't snitch. I did not tell on Rich or Alpo. I did not identify my supplier or anyone else in the game. *I didn't even tell them what my attacker did for a living*. How would telling on my shooter get me out of trouble? According to the doctors, I was about to die. Exposing him wasn't going to take the bullets out or bring anybody back to life. If anybody was a snitch, it was the guy who'd set me up because he told on his two boys!

Any cat who wants to make me feel bad for identifying the cat who shot me is in my opinion ignorant. Anybody who says I violated the street code is a fool. Until somebody walks in my shoes and has seen death face-to-face, they're not in a position to question my judgment. Was I supposed to let this cat just get away with murdering some of my closest friends? Was I supposed to just die and let these cats go unpunished?

An issue of *Don Diva* magazine, which calls itself the "original street bible," featured an article about a cat named Kevin Chiles. These days, Chiles produces *Don Diva* magazine. Back in the eighties and nineties, he was a Harlem hustler like me. Apparently, the article gave the impression that I had something to do with providing evidence used to arrest Chiles. This is my side of the story.

One day in 1991, I ran into Gangsta Lou, a friend of mine and fellow member of MobStyle, the rap group I formed. Lou told me he'd attended the "Jack the Rapper" convention, a convention for new and seasoned rap artists to showcase their talents and market their music. He mentioned that a guy we'll call BT was on his bus. BT was apparently dealing with another hustler in Harlem named Kevin Chiles. Kevin wanted to break into the music industry.

I'd already had run ins with BT, and strongly believed he was an undercover cop. I asked Lou if he gave Kevin Chiles the scoop on BT. Lou said he didn't because he didn't want to start any trouble based on hearsay.

Snitching

By this time, I wanted to do a movie about my life. I wanted to ask Alpo some questions for the movie, so we spoke on the phone while he was locked up. I also needed him to sign some forms giving me legal permission to discuss him in the movie.

'Po mailed me the consent forms and sent me another package. The package contained several papers discussing 'Po's trial and the upcoming case against Kevin Chiles. The papers indicated that the cops were building a case against Chiles's organization.

Shortly after I received that package, I ran into a cat named C from Mount Vernon, who was affiliated with Kevin. I arranged a time to give him the papers Alpo sent me. I wanted to warn him and Kevin that the feds were coming after them. I'd want someone to do the same for me.

I don't know if Kevin ever read the papers thoroughly, but if he did, he would know that BT was a government informant. It was in the document. BT presented himself as a music producer to get into Kevin's circle, arranged some drug deals, and then began supplying the feds with information to indict Kevin, the same game he tried to run on me.

Somehow, my passing information on to Kevin in an effort to warn him was interpreted as me telling on Kevin! If I was working with law enforcement to arrest him, why would I warn him? Ironically, allegations came out that Kevin's boy C turned state witness against Kevin to reduce his own sentence.

I don't blame Kevin for this misunderstanding. Someone obviously wanted to cause problems between us. Whoever implied that I snitched on Kevin was misinformed.

I am aware of Kevin's background, and my heart goes out to him. His mother was savagely killed in her home because of Kevin's involvement in the game. I hope that Kevin learned from the past just as I did; his eyes should water when he thinks about all the lives destroyed in the game. His mother was an innocent victim. Tragedies like those remind us that the game is over. It's not about competing to see who sold more coke, or who had more women, or who laundered their money the best.

To be honest, I never wasted a lot of time worrying about snitches. The real question people should ask is: "Who creates snitches?" Members of law enforcement who want a break in their cases create the demand for snitches. Prosecutors offer a lighter sentence if a defendant testifies against someone else or drops a name.

The problem with this is that defendants often lie just to get a reduced sentence. "Give us some names and we might be able to reduce your sentence." Some people snitch on their partners, and then give names of people who have nothing to do with the crime!

The first law of nature is self-preservation. Many people will fuck up another man's life to preserve his or her own. This means there are possibly thousands of people doing time unfairly. Where is the justice in that? Does the prosecution care? No, they just want to win their case. This is just another example of injustice in the so-called criminal justice system.

Snitching

Everybody in the 'hood is paranoid about being ratted out, or snitched on. Certain street magazines make matters worse when they use snitch stories to sell copies. The publishers of such magazines tend to be cats who want to live through the lives of hustlers and gangsters. They know people are interested in nostalgic tales of former criminals, so they feed it to the people. The average person reading is fascinated by these stories, and becomes *more* curious about street life.

By the way, has anyone stopped to think that maybe *federal agents read these magazines*? You call yourself telling on snitches or keeping it real, and meanwhile you're supplying the feds with more misinformation to build half-baked cases against cats. Writers for these magazines should be careful how they talk about snitches, because *they* might be snitches on the low.

When people get in trouble, they always blame someone or something outside of themselves. Hustlers have to take responsibility for their acts. They have to know and accept the consequences of the choices they make. Wise men know that much of their success or failure in life comes from their own thoughts and actions.

Check this scenario out. You wear $50,000 of jewelry, have ten to fifteen luxury cars, wear expensive minks, and keep no less than $10,000 in your pockets at all times. You spend thousands on clothes then go to parties to floss for girls. You take pictures, posing with guns, and make sure to blast your music as you drive down the block. You cause scenes everywhere you go to get attention. You buy fancy homes or rent fancy apartments right by your headquarters. You give girls you just met money to go shopping, and sometimes pay their rent. You get locked up and immediately start thinking about who ratted on you, and who's working with the jakes, or police.

You come up with a list of possible snitches, but leave the most important person's name off the list: Yours! Let's keep it real. You snitch on yourself every time you act too flashy. You give cops all the clues they need to investigate you. After all, you got all that shit, with no legitimate job.

When you do cats dirty by coming up short with their money, or not giving them a fair percentage, you cloud a dude's head with revenge and envy. When you sleep with some gold-digger chick and let her know your business, you set yourself up to fall. That same chick might be sexing some of the cops who patrol your turf (yes, it happens!) or rival dealers.

All it takes is a few words spoken to the wrong people at the wrong time, and your so-called drug empire is finished. You don't spend time helping your team understand their roles and their importance to the whole operation. You don't share profits. You don't have your team's back. A dude pitching coke for you catches a case and you refuse to bail him out.

It's easy to blame your failure on other cats. The truth is that your shit failed not just because of some snitch, but because you didn't take the time to get everybody on the same page. You didn't make sure *everybody* was eating. Instead of looking at the big picture, you focus on self, and forget about your boys.

Many brothers in America's prisons receive subscriptions to various street magazines. Some of these cats on lockdown got there through drug-related offenses. Some of these cats want to relive the days when they were getting money. Hopefully these brothers will be careful not to fill their minds with the negative ideas that took their freedom in the first place.

When I came home from the hospital in '87, Rich and Alpo gave me the 411 about the streets. Rich had a new drug connection, a cat named Fritz from 112th Street. Rich and Alpo were now into the crack game, which made far more money than regular cocaine. Alpo made regular trips copping bricks in Virginia, Baltimore, and D.C.

We didn't spend any time with regrets or tragedy. We laughed and joked to keep the mood light. They gave me the update about new cars they copped and the new homes they purchased.

I remember both of them sported Rolex watches and other nice jewelry. Things had changed within the last two months. They were getting paid more than ever, going on trips, and escorting some beautiful ladies. They already ran through all the fly girls in Harlem; at this point, they became interstate players, transporting girls in from different states. These sisters had exotic haircuts, beautiful flawless skin, and perfect figures. The game went on without me, and my boys were the talk of the town.

A few days after I got home, Lulu stopped by with a duffel bag full of coke. I tried to tell him that I wasn't ready to dive back into the ice. I needed a break from the game.

"No, Azito. This is for you, my friend. Just get back

what they took from you. I give this to you, my friend. No cost. I love you."

"Naw, Lu, I'm gonna leave that shit alone. I gotta get right with God, know what I mean?"

"Me too, Azito. I gonna leave this shit alone too. My wife has child now and we move soon. Me have nice house in Santo Domingo . . . big hotel and gas station too. I leave this shit alone after what I see happen to you, Azito. I don't take chances on life no more. My wife scared for me, you know? I see the light, Azito. No more for me. I got one last package, then I go."

I actually saw the sincerity in his eyes. "You get better, Azito," he said as he hugged me tightly and kissed me on the head.

As he left, I thought, "Something must have got into Lulu, I never heard him talk like that." I was glad for him. He made a wise and noble decision. I thought it took a lot of strength to leave the game like that and move on with his life.

But Lulu's decision came too late. He never got a chance to knock off that last package. A client he supplied gunned Lulu down. His wife left for Santo Domingo when she received the news, never to return.

It was time to take the cast off my leg. When I first went outside, the police rolled right up on me. "Hey, Azie, how you doing," they asked while patting me down. The cops took turns cracking jokes on me. "What did you get shot with, a water gun?" "Come on, Superman, you can tell me. You got shot in the head and lived. I guess it pays to have a big fuckin' head, huh, Azie?"

Snitching

I grabbed my dick and said, "Yeah, how do you know?" The officer threw me against the wall, ready to attack. The captain called him off me and told me to leave and be careful. I had a second chance now, and I didn't intend to blow it.

12

The Crucifixion

People usually associate crucifixion with Jesus Christ. However, crucifixion can also refer to an act of violence directed against any innocent person. Their murder becomes a rallying cry against wicked and shameful acts, and the victim becomes a martyr. I could not recognize it at the time, but our prominence in Harlem as drug dealers led to a crucifixion.

Around 1990, my boy Rich found himself floating in a sea of problems. We sat down and had a long conversation in his sixteen-valve Benz one day. He was tired of hustling. "I'm taking too many losses," he told me. He'd let his friend Black Just, from Queens, borrow his Porsche 944. The police pulled Just over one night and seized Rich's car. According to Rich, they threatened to keep his car forever.

"My little chick from the projects is under investigation," he told me. "That Porsche is in her name and she's scared to death."

Game Over

He revealed his plan to buy a house in Florida. "This is no place to live. I don't want my family growing up around this bullshit no more." Rich believed cats were jealous of him because he was such a good "chef."

Rich cooked crack quickly and profited faster than most other hustlers. He had the best prices on the street and blew away all competition. He sold jumbos two for five dollars, and had long cheese lines wrapped around his spots all day and night. "When my crew is out, nobody else gets paid. I got that butter shit," he boasted.

"Yo, Rich, you gotta eat and let eat," I advised.

But Rich wasn't having it. "Fuck that nice guy shit! Nice guys finish last. I need *all* this paper. I'm not trying to be in this shit forever." I wanted Rich to slow down. His mind was racing a hundred miles an hour, going downhill with no brakes.

"Yo, A, you're not going to believe this one," Rich continued. "I'm having so much bad luck. The fucking cops pulled me over the other night. I was driving my cousin's Nissan Maxima, and I had forty grand cash on me. They took all my information and gave me a voucher slip for the cash. To get my money back, I got to bring them proof of where I got the money from."

"Yo, dog, sounds like they on you. You got to chill," I said.

"Then the other day, they ran up in my stash house and found like a hundred grand in singles. Lucky for me, no one was in there."

I heard enough of my boy's problems to know he needed to drop the drug hustle and find a new one. I had begun to see hip-hop as a way out of dealing drugs, and I wanted Rich to join me.

"Yo, Rich, why don't you leave this drug shit alone and get with this rap shit? I'm going to start a group, and it's gonna blow," I said with enthusiasm.

"Nigga, I can't rap! Picture me, Rich Porter, rapping," he replied. "Yo, A, let me finish telling you my story." Rich couldn't see the big picture. Our popularity on the streets was so crazy that people would have accepted anything we did.

"People will support us, trust me. Let's go legit. We owe this to them. Plus, from the look of things it sounds like you are running out of time." Rich still wasn't trying to hear me. He did not recognize that we were shepherds and our followers were the sheep. In the heart of the big apple, we were the Harlem trendsetters.

Rich dismissed my ideas about music and continued talking. He told me about how he sent Alpo to do a deal with some Dominican cats on Broadway. Alpo had $150,000 on him. The Dominicans told him to wait in the living room and they'd bring back the product. While Alpo waited, they snuck out the window with Rich's cash!

"Yo, A, it's crazy! And my mom still gets high. I don't want Donnell to be around this shit. Plus, he can play ball real good—him and my nephew Trav. Maybe they can make it to the NBA, who knows?"

Rich went on talking about having two kids on the way by two different girls. He was stressed.

"Yo, Dick, you got to take a trip before you go crazy," I advised.

"I feel you, Z . . . with the music, I mean. It's a good idea."

"Thanks, man. This shit ain't easy. It ain't no walk in the park. Seems like it ain't about what you know, but who you know in the music game."

Rich suggested I go to New Jersey and talk to his man Leland Robinson. Leland's mother and father created Sugar Hill Records, the first label to put hip-hop on wax. They also recorded rap's first huge hit, "Rapper's Delight."

"That record sold like seventeen million copies," Rich reminded me. "The Robinsons are living large, A. They got Ferraris, a Rolls-Royce, and a mansion out of this world!"

"Yo Rich, that's real talk, why didn't I think of that?" It was good advice. But I couldn't shake the feeling that Rich was digging himself into a deep hole. To make matters worse, it seemed like the police were right on his heels.

After talking, we pulled up to Willie Burgers. Tons of people were on the block when we arrived. It was as if they were waiting for us. Even the cook seemed to stop and flip burgers in slow motion as we pulled up. The Benz attracted everyone's attention and we felt like Hollywood superstars.

Eventually I followed Rich's advice and went to New Jersey searching for Leland Robinson. I heard he chilled out in a roller rink, so that's where I went. Lou and I pulled up in a Benz wagon. It was mad crowded that night. We probably got there too late because everybody was leaving.

We left and headed back to New York City, doing at

least a hundred miles per hour on the highway. I slowed down because I sensed a serious accident about to happen. All of a sudden, I heard a loud noise—*BOOM!* All we saw was a huge cloud of smoke. As things began to clear up, we saw two cars turned completely over.

We pulled over and got out, only to see two girls that we knew from Harlem. Both were dead. One car had literally wrapped around a pole. It hurt me to see this girl dead, most likely from racing with other cats.

Tragedy hit again, real hard. This time it was personal. Pat was mad at me because I'd left her at my mom's house for several days. I called over there looking for her. I was cheating and I felt guilty. Usually when I got caught or if she was suspicious, she would go crazy.

Something was different this time. She was serious, but very calm when she spoke. "Azie, my mother called and said Donnell didn't come home from school yet and it's like six o'clock. He's usually home by now. I'm going to my mother's house, I'll see you later," Pat said as she abruptly hung up the phone.

I jumped in my car and raced over to my mother's house. Still feeling guilty, I thought Pat had enough of my lying and had finally decided to leave me. Maybe the whole story about Donnell was just an excuse for her to bounce, I thought. But when I got there Pat was gone. My mother said she left right after getting off the phone with me. "Azie, I think Donnell is missing," she said.

I tried to call Pat's mom to see if everything was alright. Ms. Porter picked up the phone yelling and began cursing me out. I hadn't even said a word yet.

"Motherfucker, don't play with me. Where is my son?"

"Velma, this is Azie," I said, a little shocked at her words. She handed the phone to Pat and I asked, "This shit is real? Your brother didn't come home yet?"

"No," Pat responded. "And some man just called saying he got Donnell and wanted to talk to Richard."

"Where is Rich?" I asked.

"He's on his way over here now."

"Yo, Pat, I'm on my way too. I'll be right there."

When I got there, Rich had arrived and he was visibly upset. His left leg trembled and he kept shaking his head in disbelief. Meanwhile, his mother was screaming, "I hope you don't owe nobody money out there. If you do you better pay them, because I want my son home *now*! My son don't got shit to do with this," Ms. Porter said. "Nothing better happen to my son!" Pat did her best to calm her mother.

Suddenly the phone rang, and Rich answered it. I held my ear to the phone as well. No sooner had Rich said, "Hello," than the voice on the other end said, "Yeah, Rich, we want five hundred thousand."

Rich was like, "Yo, don't do nothing to my little brother. I don't have no five hundred thousand. I'm going to kill you, motherfucker!"

The voice replied, "Oh, you want to play games," and they hung up the phone.

I warned Rich not to talk to them too hard since they had the upper hand. He slammed the phone down, saying, "Fuck that!" He couldn't recognize the voice on the phone, and he didn't have a clue concerning Donnell's whereabouts. The scene was crazy. Ms. Porter was crying and yelling at the top of her lungs, Pat was crying, and by now, Rich began to shed some tears too.

I didn't know what to do. All I could say was "Yo, if they call back tell them to give you enough time to get the money. Don't flip on them like that no more, they might do something stupid." Just the thought of harm coming to Donnell got Rich heated. "They better not hurt my little brother," he angrily replied. He went toward the back of the apartment, found his gun, and put it in his waistband.

At that moment, the doorbell rang. It was Rich's uncle, Johnny, also known as Apple.

"Velma, what's going on here? Why is everybody so sad?"

"Somebody kidnapped Donnell," she replied. "They got my baby and they want five hundred thousand dollars, Johnny . . . a half million dollars! I'm calling the cops. I want my baby back!"

"No, slow down. Don't do that," Apple pleaded. "Rich what's going on here? What is your mother talking about? You don't know who it could be? Now, what did they—" The phone rang again, interrupting Apple. Rich picked it up in a hurry.

"Yo, playboy, you got that cash or what?" the kidnapper asked.

Rich was boiling by now and he barked back, "I told y'all, I don't have no money and you better not hurt my brother!" That's when things took a turn for the worse. The voice on the other end said, "Listen, the ball is in our court and it's time for you to listen to us. We want the money and we know you got it. Don't make this difficult, motherfucker!"

The kidnapper suddenly hung up the phone. Apple pulled his angry nephew aside and started talking to him. I guess the news traveled through the grapevine, because soon, everybody and their mother knew about Donnell's kidnapping. Within minutes, the apartment was packed with concerned troops.

I was dazed and upset. My mind was racing as I tried to figure out who was behind the kidnapping. I asked God for insight, and then I walked outside so I could think. Immediately, I focused on a few pieces of information. My first thought was that Apple ran with a dude named Preacher and a group of cats who exhorted hustlers in Harlem. My second thought was that Rich brought boxes of coke to his mom's house on the regular. He cooked the coke so crazy that he got an extra five hundred grams per key. He got cocaine for such a good price that he was able to sell it wholesale for tremendous profit. His uncle Apple lived in the same household, so he saw firsthand how Rich got down. It seemed a little crazy, but Rich and his uncle could be my major suspects. But Rich was real close to his uncle, so I quickly dismissed the thought. Nah, he wouldn't do that, I thought.

I went upstairs to check on Pat. I knew she was stressing.

"You alright, Pat?"

"I just want my little brother back," she said with desperation. "I swear to God if I get my little brother back,

I'm leaving all this bullshit alone. Y'all making all this money, buying cars, flossing mad jewelry, fucking all these wack bitches, fucking niggas' wives and niggas' sisters; maybe somebody is jealous. Maybe somebody wants revenge. I am so tired of this bullshit; I have nightmares all the time. I told you and Richard, I wanted to get my brother out of here," she said, in tears. "Please, God, let him come home safe!"

I realized Pat was right. I remembered one day the crew stood on the corner chilling, and some cats pulled up and started firing shots at me, Alpo, and Rich. They started taunting us, "Fuck y'all, you ain't all that, fuck you, pussies." I never knew who it was. Just like Pat said, all our bullshit was bound to come back one way or another. I just wished Donnell didn't have to be affected by what we did.

Pat asked, "Where's Alpo? I guess he's out of town, huh? I told you I wanted to get my little brother out of here. I knew something was going to happen. I'm going back downstairs," she said with a sigh.

We joined the family and friends downstairs just as the phone rang again. "So you wanna play games, motherfucker? Go to McDonald's on 125th Street and Broadway and look under the sink in the men's bathroom. There's a package there for you." When they hung up, Rich sent Stan to the location.

Stan returned saying he didn't find anything, so we waited for the kidnappers to call back. We suspected that Stan might have been afraid to go. This cat named Kevin brought his telephone by the house. It had caller ID, which would allow us to get the caller's number and find out their location. The phone didn't work and the calls stopped, so everybody started raising some money in an effort to bring Donnell back.

They called again saying, "You see it's not a joke, right? We want the money now! We don't want to kill him." Rich told them we didn't find anything. The kidnapper told Rich to go back and look again. Rich and his cousin Nut rushed to the McDonald's and came back with the package. Tears flowed freely down Rich's face. He showed us the bag containing one of Donnell's fingers, his name ring, and a cassette tape.

We played the tape and heard Donnell pleading for his young life. "Mommy, I don't want to die, please help! Tell Richard to give them the money," he begged, in obvious pain. "Mommy, I love you, tell Pat I love her too. Help me, Mommy. Please don't let them kill me. They cut my finger off. Mommy, it hurts real bad, and it won't stop bleeding. Help me, please!"

Pat heard this and went crazy. Nut put the severed finger back into the bag along with Donnell's ring. Pat grabbed the bag, grabbed the tape, and ran out the door, headed straight for the precinct, yelling, "No!" Apple tried his best to catch her, but Pat was gone. She ran so fast it seemed like she flew out of the door. That whole scenario was the saddest thing I ever witnessed.

Once Pat involved the police, the incident made the headlines of New York City newspapers and television news programs. Because Donnell was kidnapped, the FBI got involved and sent undercover agents over to tap the phones. But the kidnappers never called back. That's when I knew it was someone right around us who had masterminded the plot—someone in our midst.

A few days passed with no phone calls from the kidnappers. Apple told Rich that someone slid a letter underneath his aunt's door:

"He's still alive. We still want the money. He needs to be in the hospital. He lost a lot of blood. He is getting weak. We know the pigs are involved. Be wise. This is your last chance. Go to phone on the corner of 207th Street and Sherman Avenue, we are going to call you, come alone, at nine o'clock sharp."

Rich and his uncle spoke in the hallway. The feds were still in the apartment waiting for a call.

Apple was like, "Come on, man, we can do this. Let's get your brother back. These feds don't give a fuck about you or Donnell. They just want to build up a case on all of us, so that they can bring us down. Can't you see?" Rich looked at the letter and then looked seriously at his uncle. He went inside the apartment and handed the letter over to the feds.

The feds suggested Rich follow directions and go to the designated spot for the call. The agents staked the spot out and wired the phone. At nine o'clock, no one called. Rich stayed by the phone for about an hour, and still the kidnappers never called.

Fritz, Rich's drug supplier, came by to see Rich. Fritz was a great person with a lot of cash, and he was very powerful in Harlem. Years later, he contracted AIDS from a blood transfusion following a gunshot wound. He told me that personally.

"Hold your head up, man," Fritz said to Rich. "I'll do whatever I have to do to get your brother back. Come through the spot tomorrow and I'll give you thirty bricks. Just use that to get your brother back, I don't want a dime," he said.

Rich called on Alpo to sell the bricks out of town because he was hot. The feds had their eyes on him. Rich wasn't trying to get caught transporting huge quantities of cocaine across state borders with his brother missing.

I was riding in my Volkswagen Corrado, with heavily tinted windows, about a week or two after Donnell's kidnapping, when I saw Rich walking down St. Nick Avenue. I pulled up, rolled the window down, and called his name. He was so startled that he jumped back and pulled out his gun. I pulled the window down all the way, so he could see that it was me. He breathed a sigh of relief and jumped in my ride.

"Yo, Dick, where you heading," I asked.

"Back to my mom's house," Rich replied.

Rich was clearly paranoid and nervous. He wore a bulletproof vest, and showed me two nine-millimeter handguns he carried. He looked like Rambo, ready to go to war. He admitted he was paranoid and that he felt he couldn't trust anybody.

It was all his fault, Rich confessed, admitting that his lifestyle had caught up to him. Rich was in confession mode. He told me how he did some foul shit to his man DB. He got DB's little brother murdered because of his disrespectful conduct with crack fiends. This dude got over on the customers by selling them pieces of soap in crack vials.

The Crucifixion

The little brother actually smoked crack himself and would do anything to get high—including smoking his product. This fucked up Rich's business, because the crackheads kept complaining that the dealer was cheating them. Rich got dudes to rough him up a few times as a warning. DB's brother kept using the product and cheating the customers despite the warnings. Rich admitted that he lost patience with the cat, and had him killed. For years I thought that someone he cheated had killed him.

Rich felt like all that shit had come back to haunt him. There was nowhere to run or hide. Still shocked by what I just heard, I tried to calm Rich down and talk to him.

"Yo, Rich, you got to ask God to forgive you."

"God? Nah, man, God don't give a fuck about me," Rich said. "The streets took care of me all my life, not my mother or my father . . . just me, hustling! I've been doing this ever since I was thirteen years old. I can't turn back now."

"Yo, Rich, we left God, but He would never leave us." Rich was through with the conversation. He asked me to drop him off at 132nd Street and Seventh.

"Tell God to get my little brother back," he said sarcastically.

"Yo, Rich, there *is* a God."

"I know, A, but I guess it's time for me to pay. Thou shall not kill—the fifth commandment. It's too late." We pulled up to the spot. Rich got out and told me he'd see me later. This was January of 1990.

A few nights later, my crew and I played basketball on 122nd Street and Second Avenue, right by the FDR highway. My man Sherman was there, along with Lou, Mook, and Prince. We heard a gunshot on the highway. I thought, Somebody just lost their life, and the thought took something out of me. It felt crazy. Lou pointed to the spot he thought the shot came from. We continued playing and I had a good series of games, busting their ass, hitting three-pointers from every angle of the court.

We jumped in the car and drove back to headquarters on 132nd Street, where we hung out and talked shit about the game. I noticed a Suzuki jeep roll by slowly across the street. I looked and said, "That looks like Alpo," but Lou reminded me that 'Po "wouldn't be driving no wack shit like that." I insisted Alpo was the driver, and as I raised my hand to get his attention, the jeep made a U-turn and stopped right in front of us.

Alpo and a friend jumped out of the jeep and slapped everybody five. He introduced his boy as "Wayne from D.C." Then Alpo asked if I had seen Rich. I glanced down at my watch and told Alpo, "You know Rich don't be out this late." Everybody knew that Rich went to sleep early and woke up early like clockwork. I told 'Po what Rich used to tell me: "He's a day person, not a night person. That's how he's able to stay alert and in control."

Alpo quickly agreed, but I knew something wasn't right. He had some very deep scratches on his face that were still bleeding. I inquired about the scratches and he said, "Oh, me and my bitch back in D.C. had a little fight." I was skeptical about that answer so I was like, "Word . . . in D.C.? But you still bleeding, homey." Before Alpo could explain, a kid named Travis flew past us in his ride. Alpo and his man Wayne jumped back in the jeep and 'Po said, "Yo, I got to catch this dude, but I'll be right back." With that, he pulled off. The whole thing was strange—'Po driving that wack car, asking about Rich, the scratches on his face, and the way he just took off like that.

My man Sherm shared my uneasy feelings about what just happened. He said "Yo, something ain't right about 'Po. I'm not feeling that cat right now. Well, anyway, I'm going upstairs. Be careful, Z."

Shortly after 'Po broke out, a girl I knew walked up and indicated she wanted to chill with me. I threw her my car key and told my people I'd see them later. The girl mentioned that she was hungry and suggested we grab a bite to eat. I was tired from playing ball, so I let her drive.

I told her that I planned to take her to a hotel after eating. She was like, "Fuck the hotel, let's go to my house. I could use that money." We arrived at White Castle—the one by Fordham Road and Webster Avenue in the Bronx. It was convenient since homegirl lived in that area.

My beeper went off like crazy, displaying 911 on the screen. I knew it was my mom, sending me an emergency page. I jumped out the car and called her.

"Yeah, Mom, what is it?"

"You know they found Pat's brother dead, right?"

"I had a feeling something happened. It's been a while since they took him. That's crazy," I said, feeling instantly depressed.

"Where are you, Azie?"

"I'm going into White Castle, Ma. Let me call Pat—that's her beeping me now."

Game Over

Pat was in tears when I called her. I knew she was hurting and I could only imagine how Rich would react when he found out.

"I heard the bad news, Pat. I'll be right there. Did you speak to Rich yet, does he know about Donnell?" I asked.

"Azie, *Richard was killed, not Donnell.*"

The phone fell from my hand, and in a split second, my mind traveled back to that gunshot I'd heard by the park earlier that night. Just a few nights earlier, Rich and I had that deep conversation that we thought we'd continue later. I never knew that would be the last time I would see my man Rich Porter.

I didn't even bother to continue the conversation. The pain of Rich's death was too much for me, and I didn't want to hear any more details. I returned to the pretty girl waiting for me by the drive-through window of White Castle. I was no longer in the mood to fuck.

"What's wrong, baby, what's wrong?" she asked.

"Nothing," I said. "Just get your food and let's be outta here." When we got to her apartment, I jumped right in the bed. I tried to pull the covers over me and get some sleep, but I kept seeing images that disturbed me.

Over and over that night, I woke up to the same dream: Rich and Donnell smiling and playing like they were on vacation. I thought I was going crazy. I went back to sleep, and I didn't wake up till six p.m. the next day.

I gave homegirl a few thousand dollars and made my way to the block. When I arrived, it seemed like everybody and their mother was there. My man TM was the first one to greet me, visibly upset. When Alpo arrived, he got out his car crying. "Yo, what happened to Rich? No, man, no . . . somebody got to die," he exclaimed before jumping back into his car and taking off.

My man TM announced, "Yo, we got to kill him. Alpo killed Rich. I know you know that, A. You know him better than anybody." I tried to calm him down, but he demanded to be heard. "We can't let him get away with killing Rich. If you don't move, I will."

"Yo, killing is not the way. God is trying to tell us something," I said.

"Try telling that to Alpo. I bet he'll put a hole in your fucking head. Fuck that, he got to go." He left in tears, refusing to hear what I had to say.

Alpo never came back around. He didn't attend the wake or the funeral at Benta's, yet his name was signed in Rich's funeral book, which was suspicious. About a month after cops found Rich's body, the Porter family received more tragic news: the cops found Donnell's little lifeless body in Orchard Beach, the same area where they'd found Rich's body.

The detectives said an old homeless man looking for cans found him wrapped in fourteen garbage bags. Pat told me that she met the old man. On the day of Donnell's funeral, she spotted the old man standing right across the street from the funeral parlor. My mind was blown.

At that point, I asked God to show me a sign. Two days after Donnell's funeral I stood on the block where he and Rich grew up. Right there on 132nd Street, a big beautiful rainbow appeared in the sky. I happened to be speaking with Alex, the picture man, when I spotted the sign I'd asked for. "Yo, Alex, you got to take a picture of this rainbow. This is the hand and the voice of God."

He took out the camera and snapped the most amazing picture. Looking at it sent my thoughts into another dimension. The appearance of that rainbow let me know for sure that Rich and Donnell made it into heaven. It also told me that God wanted the drug game to come to a permanent end. My sadness melted away when I saw that rainbow, and I was at peace.

My peace lasted for about a week. I soon learned that my man Stan had been murdered. I'd known Stanley Harvey since we were kids. Stan always got into some shit. One time he stuck his hand in an icemaker and damn near lost his finger.

When I began hustling, Stan wanted to get down so bad, but his mom, Ms. Virginia, wasn't having it. She owned the neighborhood Laundromat, and his pop was a retired police officer. I'm pretty sure they made a good household income, so Stan really didn't need to hustle. But he did so anyway. The first time I gave Stan some work, his mom found the drugs and threw them in the garbage. Then she called my mother and told her to keep me away from her son.

She had a good reason for feeling this way because of a prior incident. My sister Robin had a boyfriend who gave me a .22-caliber handgun. Stan and I walked up the hill on 145th Street between Convent and Amsterdam. I showed Stan my gun, and he said it wasn't real. I insisted it was and he tried to grab it from me to see for himself. There we were, both grabbing at the gun, when it misfired and shot Stan in the leg!

Stan started to yell, "You shot me . . . you shot me!" An old man across the street from us yelled at me, "Hey, put down the gun. I saw you shoot that boy." I got so nervous that I ran back down the hill fast as I could. I heard the old man in the distance yelling, "Somebody catch him! He shot that boy."

I was so scared I didn't know what to do. I went home and changed my clothes. I threw on a trench coat and went back up the hill in disguise, hoping that no one would recognize me. When I got back to the scene of the crime no one was there. I went walking back home thinking to myself, "I hope he's alright." I quickly dismissed the idea that I was a murder suspect when I realized he wasn't dead!

I didn't see Stan and I got worried—not just for my safety, but also for his. A couple of hours later, after tossing and turning in my bed that night, the doorbell rang loudly. I pretended I was asleep. I feared it was the cops. Remembering the gun was in my pocket, I jumped up and threw the pistol on top of the closet. My sister answered the door. It was Stan's mom, Ms. Virginia! I just knew I was a dead man. My mother was tight about someone ringing her bell late at night. I knew she'd be even more upset when she learned about the shooting incident.

"Mom," my sister said, "it's important." My mother gave my sister permission to open the door and in walked Ms. Virginia. She sat in the living room and spoke with my mother for a few minutes before I heard my mom scream, "Get that motherfucker in here right now." At this point, my funeral was just minutes away, as soon as Ms. Virgina left, I thought.

My sister came in my room trying to wake me. I continued to act like I was asleep; I did not want to go out there and confront both my mom and Stan's. My mother didn't go for it. "Get in here before I come back there and kill you."

That was the longest walk I ever had to take. Ms. Virginia immediately asked me where I got the gun. I lied and told her I found it. My mother slapped the shit out of me so hard I had to pick it up with toilet paper. My mother and father kicked my ass all over the place that night. At one point, my father held me down while my mother spanked my naked ass.

My mother made me apologize to Ms. Virginia. "Please forgive me before they kill me," I said. Ms. Virginia told me I was lucky Stanley didn't tell on me. Stanley actually told the cops that somebody else shot him. I explained to my mother and Ms. Virginia that I didn't shoot Stan. He tried to grab the gun from me and it went off by accident.

"Y'all shouldn't be playing with no gun anyway. What if you would have killed my son?" she asked. My mother pressured me to confess the source of my gun, but I stuck with the lie that I found it. The cat had given me the gun to protect myself from a school bully. Ms. Virgina was right. I could have accidentally killed Stanley that night.

The Crucifixion

I never got a chance to tell Stan I loved him. Stan didn't deserve to die. He wasn't one to provoke conflict. The last time I saw Stan he'd expressed the urge to avenge Rich's murder. I tried to convince him that the game was over for us. I advised Stan to stay off the block and let things cool off, but he didn't take my advice. Stanley was found dead on a roof of an abandoned building in 1990. He was my best friend and I still miss him.

Pat called me about a week after Donnell's body was found and told me that her father was hit by a car and killed. A hit-and-run? Pat just lost her only two brothers, now she'd lost her father. I didn't leave my house for days after that. I didn't want to hear evil or see evil. I didn't even wash my car, which I always kept perfectly clean, for weeks.

A few days later, I went downstairs to get something out of the trunk of my car. I stopped in my tracks when I read the note some fool scribbled in the dirt on my car: "You're next, motherfucker!" The devil was working very hard to clip my wings. I maintained a low profile for a while because I didn't know where all this negative energy was coming from.

I didn't want to be Batman anymore. I wanted my job back at the cleaners. I did everything possible to stay low and avoid attention. I continued to stay away from parties. I believed that if I was out of sight, I would be out of everyone's mind.

It seemed like the youth had lost their minds. Young cats killed one another left and right due to envy, jealousy, stealing, lust, adultery, competition, confusion, and mistrust. No one saw the signs. No one would listen. Everybody was in too deep, trying to be the next Azie, Rich Porter, or Alpo. All the tragedy we experienced should have made even the most wicked man see that it was time to repent. The crucifixion of innocent Donnell William Porter should have pointed people in God's direction.

Donnell's murder, along with all the others, demonstrated that there is no love in the drug game. I was shot and almost killed by someone I once employed and looked out for. Rich's close friend and business partner murdered him. Donnell's kidnapping and murder were organized by his own uncle. If these tragedies don't show how evil and destructive the drug game is, nothing will. People saw the deaths of Rich and Donnell, but didn't see how they were connected to others. When Rich died, a brother was lost, a son, an uncle, and more. An entire family was affected. When Donnell died, a son, brother, and the future was lost.

Donnell's murder helped me see the role I played in seducing youth into the drug game. We flaunted pretty women, luxurious cars, and knots of money for everyone to see. To us, these were signs of street status. I began playing the game to provide for my family and myself in ways that welfare and my parents could not, and earned lots of money and street fame in the process.

We influenced countless youth to see drug selling and violence as the only tickets out of poverty. The materialism we displayed led hip-hop artists to waste money on jewelry, cars, designer clothes, and fancy gadgets. Sadly, it took my near-death experience and the callous murder of an innocent child for me to recognize that the drug game had corrupt players, corrupt referees, and unfair rules.

13
MobStyle

Rap music was corny to Harlem street hustlers back in the eighties. We felt most of the rappers were clowns talking shit they knew nothing about. They dressed funny to us and rhymed about silly shit. But regardless of what we thought, rap was popping in the streets. It seemed to be the new music of our generation.

When we realized how much money the rap cats made, they suddenly didn't seem like clowns anymore. Unlike the previous generation, when music artists had to actually play an instrument, compose music, or sing well, these rap artists got paid just to speak their minds.

I was never a serious rapper growing up. There was a deejay named Gerald who lived across the hall from me. He called himself "The Grand Shaka." Tenants in our building often complained about his music being too loud. Sometimes I would stop by, jump on the microphone, and spit some silly lyrics, just playing around.

Gerald was the first brother who told me I should take the craft seriously.

Back then, we had summer jams in Harlem where some of the hottest artists of the time performed in Sugar Hill community centers and schoolyards. I remember seeing people like Kurtis Blow, Starski, Hollywood, DJ Randy Ran, and the list goes on. Hip-hop was going on in parks all over New York City way before you could hear it on tapes, records, or the radio.

It seemed like hip-hop had a role that everybody could play. The cats who loved music, had tons of records, and had a good ear for mixing, could be deejays. People who had a "gift of gab" and knew how to get a crowd hyped could be emcees. Coordinated cats who were natural dancers could electric boogie, break dance, or pop-lock. The artistic people who could draw and paint well got into graffiti. Cats who couldn't do any of the above could be ECs (equipment carriers).

In the seventies and early eighties, the deejay got more fame and glory than the rapper. Good deejays were like street superstars back in the day. You couldn't have a party without music, so it made sense; the cats who made everybody dance got the love. Girls around the way worshipped dudes who could cut and blend music. I remember we used to steal headphones from school and wear them around our necks to front like we were deejays. We figured this would get us attention from the ladies.

Of course, deejays play the background today. Nowadays, the emcee or lyricist is the star of the show. Yesterday's deejays have now become today's hottest producers.

They do make more money than the artist, if you really look into it. Plus, they can sell their tracks to anyone for big bucks.

The first actual rap record I heard was "Rapper's Delight" by the Sugarhill Gang. The song didn't have the sophisticated flow of rap songs today, nor did it have the best production in the world. It was basically some brothers kicking some fun, storytelling-type rap over the beat from "Good Times," a popular disco record made by a group called Chic in the seventies.

This song took America by storm. In a time when there were no multimillion-dollar budgets for promotions and advertising, "Rapper's Delight" went on to sell several million records. Once that song broke the ice, cats who were rapping at little street jams were able to become recording artists.

Most of the early rap was simple and plain, feel-good rap in which cats bragged about how cool they were or about how much attention they got from the ladies. Since rap basically began in the Bronx and Harlem, most of the early rappers came from those two parts of town. As the hip-hop movement spread, brothers and sisters all over New York City caught it and ran with it.

The eighties were the golden days of rap. The music was fun, upbeat, and diverse. It seemed like everybody had their own style. As a matter of fact, biting (copying lyrics or a certain flow from another rapper) was considered a major sin when I was growing up.

As street conditions became more violent, so too did rap music. By 1989, young cats like NWA (Niggaz with Attitude) told stories about murder and gang violence in Los Angeles. A new genre of rap called gangsta rap was born.

By the mid 1990s you had Biggie and Tupac, who represented hard core rap to the fullest. East Coast cats no longer told feel-good stories. To get radio play, brothers had to kick shit about bitches, hoes, guns, murder, drugs, and jewelry. Lyrical battles turned personal and Biggie and Tupac were killed as a result. To me, gangsta rap died when Biggie and Pac were murdered. I believe it was God's sign that the era of foolish, destructive lyrics was over.

As early as '88, I took steps to create a rap group. My man Tone used to run around with a knapsack full of rhymes he wrote, so he was the first person I approached about the idea. I went looking for him, and caught up with him on the corner of 131st Street and Eighth Avenue.

"Yo, Tone, jump in. What's good . . . do you still write rhymes?"

"No doubt," Tone replied with confidence.

"I want to invest in you—you know—put you in the studio. What you think about that?"

"Bet. You know me, G, let's make it happen."

We met at Hillside Studio in New Jersey. We tried to come up with a beat or something, but it didn't work because we had no experience. I went home and began to listen to old songs, looking for a song that we could sample. I decided on a Barry White classic. I ran out and brought a Karaoke machine so I could tape the beat over and over again until it was long enough to make a song.

In '89 I wrote a song called "Mob Style," recorded it on tape, and started blasting it in my car. Cats in the street thought it was hot. My cab driver, Three-O, had access to a recording studio. He heard the song and invited me to his partner's house, where we played it for his boy Jerry Holmes. Jerry liked it and helped me record the track over. It came out hot!

One of my sisters dated a guy named Lance Hayes, who was a disc jockey for radio station WBLS at the time. He liked the song so much that he demanded a copy of the tape. Before I knew it, he got my tape in the hands of WBLS deejay Mr. Magic, who played it as a world premiere on his show. I never made any real money off our songs, but I know the tape went platinum in the 'hood. New York City loved it. Radio station 98.7 KISS-FM deejay Red Alert rocked it, and added flava by saying, "That was an uptown thing, suckers."

Red Alert, Mr. Magic, and Chuck Chillout were the top hip-hop radio personalities in New York City during the 1980s, so their support meant a lot. Lance suggested that we do an album. He had some connections in the music industry, he said, and could get us a deal. He actually got us one with Columbia Records, but then Tone signed a side deal with DEF America Records, which was Rick Rubin's label. Rubin was Russell Simmons's old partner with Def Jam Records.

Things looked promising with Columbia Records. They gave us a $300,000 advance with a guarantee of two music videos. We were on our way, I thought. No more drug dealing, no more killings. But the deal went sour once Columbia heard about Tone signing with another company, because they wanted our entire group.

Game Over

I wasn't about to let that stop me; I put the album out anyway. We called it *The Good, the Bad, and the Ugly.* Our album cover represented the drug game to the fullest: a scale with coke, an Uzi, dice, and a license plate that read "MobStyle." The streets loved the album, and record stores couldn't keep copies on the shelf. Cats bootlegged our album in the streets and made as much a twenty dollars apiece for just ten songs.

I was dating this girl named Shelly in 1990. She stopped by one night and spent the weekend with me. It was perfect timing because I needed to relax. I felt like I was going crazy. Shelly and I stayed in for a couple of days listening to soft music—Phil Collins, Peter Gabriel, Genesis, and Howard Hewitt's *Forever and Ever* album. *"Farewell, Good Friend . . ."* I loved that piece. I was trying to get my mind right, but the streets were calling. I just had to go out and find out what was happening, and when I did, police and detectives were all over the place picking people up and asking questions about the murders of Rich and Donnell.

I drove a U-Haul truck, trying to stay "out of sight, out of mind." I stopped by to visit my mom. My sister opened the door for me and the doorbell rang right after I entered. Homicide detectives paid a visit to show me some pictures and ask some questions. Just like they say on those police television shows, the detectives stated, "You can come with us to the precinct, or we can talk here." I quickly replied, "Come in, because I'm not trying to go to nobody's precinct!"

They sat in the living room and had me scan through

several pictures of recent homicide victims. They wanted to know if I knew any of them or if I knew why they were killed. I did know a few of the cats and I knew why they'd met their unfortunate fates: their hunger for money and their participation in the game. Of course I wasn't about to tell the police that.

The detectives began asking about the murders of Rich and Donnell. They wanted to show me pictures of their bodies, but I refused to look. My reluctance to view those pictures made the cops upset; they felt I was being evasive or giving them the runaround. I really wasn't. I just could not stand to see two brothers I loved in that condition.

They started to play the typical detective game. "If you don't have a good alibi for the day of these murders we'll be coming back to lock you up for a long time, with the guys that you put away for life." With that, they handed me their business cards and left my mother's apartment.

"How did they know I was here?" I asked myself out loud when they left. They probably staked out my mother's apartment for a few weeks.

My mother heard me and said, "Boy, who you talking to? You're going crazy talking to your damn self! You're hot as a firecracker! You got to stay out of my house. I'm not going to jail or getting killed for nobody," she angrily declared. "This is too much for me. My blood pressure is up and my head is hurting."

"Ma, please, I'm so sorry. Are you okay?"

"I'll be fine," she said, as she kindly walked me to the door and put me out. "Don't be running to my house. I don't want this life around me no more." I was stunned.

Game Over

What more could happen to me? This was my mother . . . my first love, the woman whom I would give and do everything for, turning her back on me.

Meanwhile, my father said nothing. "Oh, I get it," I thought. "Everybody thinks I'm some kind of snitch and she may be thinking that I'm going to get killed, and she don't want what happened in the Bronx to happen to her and the family." I couldn't be mad at her. "It's all my fault, it's all my fault, it's all my fault," were the thoughts that swirled through my head. "I wish I never sold drugs. I'm all alone. I just want to die! Why, God, why did you bring me back here? Why didn't you take me that day? Why?"

I heard this voice in my head say, "You asked to come back." At that point, I knew I was going crazy. I had no one to talk to, and no one seemed to understand. I was talking to myself, and actually answering myself. I started to get suicidal thoughts. I jumped in the U-Haul truck and vowed to never come back outside again. I figured I'd avoid eating until I starved to death.

I was mad to the point of actually hating myself. It wasn't supposed to end like this, with everybody dying. "Well, wait for me," I said to all my people killed in the game. "I'm next. Y'all are not leaving me here with all this crazy shit."

Suddenly my phone rang. I picked up and heard Shelly crying on the other end. "Don't do it, Azie! Don't do it! I was trying to call you for the longest time. I called like fifty times trying to reach you! Please don't do it," she kept pleading.

"Calm down, baby, I was at my mother's house and the phone was in the truck. Just relax."

"What's wrong with you *now?*" she said. "Please don't kill yourself."

"What are you talking about," I asked. "What are you doing in my brain?" I couldn't understand how she called me to talk me out of killing myself at the exact time I was thinking about doing it.

"Don't be mad at me, Azie. I was looking in your drawer and I found this suicide note. Please, baby, don't kill yourself!"

"Suicide note? What the hell are you talking about?" I asked.

"The letter that you left in the drawer, Azie. Please come home now," she managed to say through tears. I asked her to read the letter to me. I had no idea what letter she referred to. She read the following words:

I got somethin' to say
To the homeboy from around the way
What's goin' on
What's goin' wrong
Knocking each other off
Word is bond . . .

As Shelly tearfully read every word, it made tears roll down my eyes too.

Stop the violence
We must live in peace, in silence

Game Over

What's going on, black?
A twelve-year-old kid kidnapped
Murdered and tortured for crack . . .

"Shelly, I was just writing some thoughts down one night, that's all. What were you doing looking through my stuff, anyway?"

"Come on, Azie, let me finish." Shelly was determined to finish reading the letter.

In '87 there was a tragedy
Somethin' like this almost happened to me
But I'm alive
And two others survived.
But God bless the three that died
Myra, Joanne, and Charlie C.
Why you had to take them?
Why you couldn't take me?
Bloodbath in '87
I knew I was dead
I felt myself going to Heaven
But I learned from my mistakes
Next time I die, God, please,
Open up the gates and let me in
So I can be at peace with my friends.
Oh, Lord, oh, Lord . . .

"That's deep," she said, "Real deep. Azie, come home now. We need to talk. Look, I love you."

I told Shelly that I needed to get to the studio and lay

that track down immediately. "The 'hood needs to hear this message from God. 'What's going on, black?' is the question we need to be asking right now," I said, feeling energized.

Shelly continued to demand that I go to her house and resist the urge to commit suicide. I had to keep telling her I had no such plans. I felt so grateful for her call. To this day, Michelle (Shelly) Carvalho may not know how much I appreciate and love her for calling me that night.

I went home after I finally convinced Shelly I would not kill myself. I had to lay that song down. Within a few days, I went to the studio and recorded "What's Going On, Black." This song was a true classic. If it were up to me, it would have been the theme song for the movie *Paid in Full*, but that's another story.

This song was so real that I felt it deserved a video. I met this cat named Dwayne Coles and we shot a low-budget video for about $3,000. It wasn't the most glamorous video, but it came from the heart; it dealt with facts about a true story. Ralph McDaniels's *Video Music Box* was the only show that aired the video. In fact, McDaniels aired it every week, because he was a real dude, and he felt the pain. The entire 'hood loved that piece. I went on to do the album, which I named *Street Wise*.

It was much different from the first album, *The Good, The Bad, and The Ugly*. It was time to wake people up and take them back to a peaceful existence. MobStyle did a lot of hardcore songs, but I tried my best to put a message in each one. I never did too many so-called gangster songs, only "Live and Let Die." Even that song wasn't really gangster to me. I felt it gave insight on what would happen if people continued to play the dirty drug game—namely, they would go to jail or die.

"Crack the Mack" was another song that I wrote and for which I shot a video. I got the idea from the old James Brown classic "King Heroin." His song addressed the drug that destroyed people during his generation. My song dealt with crack because it was the deadliest drug in our generation.

MobStyle never really blew up in the music industry, but Harlem embraces our songs to this day. MobStyle produced the soundtrack to the streets of New York City during the 1980s and nineties.

Everybody in the group had a role. I laid down the street knowledge, Lou represented the thug life, Tone the Ugly (but known to the public as Pretty Tone Capone) gave some of the most ruthless, raw, uncut, and darkest lyrics ever put on wax. He was very talented, possessing one of the best flows, or deliveries, I ever heard in my life. Whip Wop was basically the baby of the bunch, talking a lot of slick gangster shit.

Shortly after I'd left messages at Leland Robinson's studio, he stopped on the block to see me. I jumped in his car and played my tape. He loved it, and later introduced me to a cat I'll call "CZ." Lee told me that CZ helped Eric B and Rakim. "You should get with this cat, Azie. I let him hear the material, and he loves it; he wants to work with you."

CZ and I started working together to get the music thing popping. The song "MobStyle" did well and continued to get airplay on KISS-FM and WBLS. MobStyle performed at a number of local spots in the late eighties and nineties. We did a few shows in the Bronx, Yonkers, and at The Rink in New Jersey, where we headlined with Jodeci and Brand Nubian. We rocked at a spot called 3-D in the Bronx, where I met Ice Cube. We also performed at a club called 2000 in Harlem. A cat named Unique threw parties there that were always off the hook. One night we rocked the stage with Das EFX, and it was all love.

Cats were in love with our music. We were on our way. I had a feeling our music was gonna blow up, and we could leave the game alone forever. I believed I could finally get my niggas off the street and help save some lives by putting some real messages in my music. In '91 I released the single "What's Going On, Black," which received critical acclaim from thugs and gangsters; they regarded it as a street classic.

I still worked with CZ trying to get my music where it needed to be. I wanted a major label to support the project. My boys constantly told me my shit was too real to get good radio play. I wasn't trying to hear that. I kept it moving, going to the studio and making shit from the heart. The stories we told were real. If my shit sold only one copy that was fine with me, fuck what anybody else thought. I kept saying to myself, "One day I'll win, I know I will. I guess it's just not time now, but God will open the gates when He sees fit."

CZ and I recorded some tracks one day in the studio. I had a little weed in my system, which really made me hear the music clearer and write better—or so I thought at the time. Out of nowhere, CZ stepped to me and was like "Yo, Z, I got someone that wants to buy some blow. He wants to spend about fifteen thousand, he's good people."

There I was in a zone, writing some deep shit, and he took it upon himself to interrupt my flow with drug talk. "Really?" I said, thrown off by the topic.

"Yeah, he's my man," CZ replied. I told him to bring the guy to the block when he was ready. I brushed him off because I didn't want to talk about that right then. I was ready to spit some lyrics. I asked the engineer to pump up the track, and then I started to flow.

"Seat belts on, nothing wrong,
sober, pull the motherfuckin' car over,
Bang Bang, Bang, a killer's gun rang a key witness,
scared to sing. God knows the trouble it may bring.
Lawyers cool with judges work out a budget
case dismissed, they don't discuss it.
Feds put a bitch in your bed give you head, recorded everything you said.
Get busted that night out at noon, dead came home too soon.
Been here all my life asked for a loan I might as well stayed home.
Korean, Chinese, Japanese come from overseas.
May I have some money please, here take anything you need.
Jamaicans, dreads, holey Pro-Keds, now plenty of gold and new threads.

Brothers wilding whoever think they'd get a gun on Rikers Island.

I don't know ask a C-O, some dough a hoe, uncut blow you know who running the show.

Poppa's got a brand new Jag, a nickel-plated mag. Black-on-black Cadillac with a rag.

The world is mine, everything going fine. Killed by somebody nine.

We shall overcome hum by a bum in the slum as he drink his rum

on the corner they got it for you police roll on the scene. Snatch up the dope fiend but

homeboy makes a way with all the green this is how it should be done.

No drugs for no one and take away all the guns and let's have fun. When are you going to realize . . . that I am streetwise."

"Damn, that's deep," CZ commented.

I quickly corrected him. "Nah, man, it ain't deep . . . it's right on the surface."

"You gonna lay that down today?"

"No doubt, you like that?"

"Yeah, that's some real-life shit," CZ replied. "Let me leave you alone so you can finish your work; it sounds good, man. Keep it up. I'll bring my man through tomorrow." When he broke out, I laid down my "Streetwise" track in the studio.

The next day at about 6:21 p.m., I pulled up on the block, listening to the track I'd just created. Seconds later a blue Nissan Maxima pulled over on the corner. CZ left his car and entered mine. I told him I finished the track, and let my speakers bump so he could hear it. He said the song sounded "like money" and that it was time to talk business. He said his man was there, and that he was ready to "do this."

"Do what?"

"You don't remember what we talked about at the studio last night . . . the fifteen gees?"

"Oh, okay. Damn, that shit slipped my mind," I answered.

BT referred to his man in the car again and said he had the money.

"Listen, I am not trying to do no business with somebody I don't know. Fuck that," I said. "*You* get the money and I'll do business with you."

He tried to tell me how long he'd known this guy, to vouch for him. I repeated what I'd said the first time and told him if he had a problem, we could just call the deal off. CZ caught himself sounding a little bit too thirsty and replied, "I hear you, my brother. I'll be right back."

CZ went back to the car to discuss the arrangement with his friend. The other dude, whom I'd never met prior to this encounter, walked over to my car. I locked the door and rolled down the window. "Come on, Azie," he whined, "I got the money right here." He lifted his jacket up to expose the cash.

I wasn't impressed. He just didn't look legit. His look and his vibe represented some other shit maybe, but definitely not the game. That cat wore an army jacket, bell-bottom jeans, a funny-ass pair of shoes, and two beepers hanging on his shoulder strap. I fell back in my car seat and immediately thought he was police. I glanced across the street and saw two white men sitting in a van. I caught them as they were trying to lean back, and I thought, "Something is wrong with this picture."

I told CZ's boy I'd be right back. "I'm going to get that for you right now. You got all the money, right?"

He assured me he did by lifting his jacket up again. The dude was too thirsty: "Come on, Azie, don't leave me out here all day, man. It's hot out here. I'm not trying to sit on the corner with all of this money. You know where I'm coming from, right?"

Yeah, I saw where he came from alright . . . the precinct! He figured me for a sucka, but the joke was on him. I drove off, and spotted three unmarked police cars following me as I glanced in my rearview mirror.

I drove to Shelly's grandmother's house and hit the horn for Shelly to come out. She came outside in her nightclothes. Meanwhile, my "escorts" pulled over behind me. Shelly got in the car, looking confused. "What's going on, A?"

I said some slick shit to her like "The sky is the limit, don't stop till you finish, baby. Come on and ride with me for a second." Homegirl wanted to change her clothes, but I wouldn't allow it. "No don't worry about that, you're coming right back," I assured her. I didn't want her to go back upstairs. They would suspect that she was down with my operation, which would have given the cops a reason to roll up in her grandmother's house. I figured they would destroy the entire house looking for drugs.

I had other plans. I drove off the block and made my way north on the Harlem River Drive. The van, accompanied by the unmarked cars, continued to tail me. I drove across the George Washington Bridge to New Jersey, got on Route 46, and kindly went to the movie theater.

We watched the entire movie in complete silence, and I didn't mention the incident to her. If the cops rolled up on us, Shelly would have no information to provide them. She was very uncomfortable throughout the whole ordeal, and she made this known with the hundreds of questions she asked during the drive from the theater. The situation made me nervous, but the last thing I wanted to do was make her panic. I gently tapped her leg and told her everything would be alright.

After the movie (I can't remember the title due to all the bullshit going on) I drove her back to her grandmother's house and gave her a few dollars. I peeped at my rearview mirror and noticed no one following me.

The streets were calling; it was time for me to get back to the block. I parked my car uptown around my mother's house, and called my personal cabdriver. Unable to reach him, I requested my backup driver, a quiet dude referred to by the number forty-six. I hopped in his luxurious Town Car and had him drop me off at the spot on 132nd Street and Seventh Avenue.

My man Tone and C-Moe were in the building, hustling and talking shit. I jumped in the conversation and gave them the 411 on what just happened. "Yo, they on me. That nigga CZ is trying to set me up, trust me."

Coca Moe said, "Damn, CZ's a cop?"

Tone said he caught a bad vibe from CZ. "I knew something was strange about that motherfucker anyway. He wanted to do too much work for us in the studio without getting paid."

As we were talking, the same cat who rolled with CZ— the funny-outfit-wearing nigga—walked into the building and was like, "What's up, Azie, I'm still ready to do this. I got the money right here," and he again lifted up his shirt, revealing the money. "What happened to you the other night?"

I told him, "What the hell are you talking about? I don't know you. There ain't no Azie in here."

Looking confused, he remained persistent: "Come on, Azie. Man, I know you . . ." He went into a roll call routine, listing different things that would refresh my memory: "BT, the half a kilo, fifteen gees, remember?" Of course I remembered. Memory wasn't the issue. The issue was I didn't trust homeboy.

My man Tone was ready to stick him up so he got at him: "You heard what he said, homeboy. Ain't no Azie in here." I whispered to Tone and C-Moe, "Let's go inside." Tone, still thinking about all that money under homeboy's shirt, whispered, "Let me get this nigga. He got a lot of paper on him." I told my boys that the dude had to be a cop. We went upstairs and entered one of the many apartments we had in the building. We stayed until they left.

I couldn't sleep that night. I was at the point of having a breakdown. The game took too much out of me. I had enough, and I wanted to leave the shit alone totally. The game didn't seem to be on my side anymore. That cat CZ was posing as a music dude but was really a cop, and he was trying to set me up.

That Sunday I pulled up on the block and saw my man Lou standing on the corner. I called him over and told him, "The sky is the limit. Don't stop till you finish. Yo, it's hot as a motherfucker out here."

He said, "Yo, your man CZ came through just a minute ago and wanted me to get him half a bird. He gave me the money, so I went uptown to see my Spanish peeps on Broadway. I got the half a brick right upstairs. I'm waiting for him to come back right now and get it."

"He gave you the money?" I asked.

"Yeah."

"And you still got the half-brick upstairs?"

"Yeah, A, what's the problem?"

"Yo, don't give him shit . . . that motherfucker is police. Listen to me. Go get that shit out of the spot and keep it, don't give him shit. That's yours, you heard?"

"Alright, fuck him, then," Lou responded. He ran upstairs to handle his business. I'd come right in the nick of time. Those motherfuckers wanted me real bad . . . damn. In the midst of my wickedness, God still had my back.

I don't know if CZ came back that night, and we sure as hell didn't stay around to find out! I do know that he never came back around the block after that day. That's the day when I really knew it was time to stop hustling. I knew that if they didn't get me, they would come after someone I knew or someone who was close to me. I didn't want anybody down with me to get locked up.

I listened closely to my intuition, that voice in my head

that always provided me with direction and clarity. Cats thought I was crazy because I constantly said, "God is good," and all I wanted to talk about was God. Street dudes didn't want to hear that. The more I talked about God, the more cats faded away and the better I began to see the Lord.

I liked this cat, CZ. He was a funny dude, cracking jokes and making me laugh all the time. Maybe the joke was really on me. He caught me sleeping up in the studio.

CZ had me going; he'd convinced me that we should open an office and we did, up in Peekskill, New York. It was a nice spot. Lou and I went to the office one day to paint. We were playing around and talking shit when all of a sudden we looked at each other and had the same thought at the same time: What if this nigga is a fed and the whole joint is bugged? We jumped up, hopped in my jeep, and drove back to Harlem.

I used to let CZ hold my Nissan Pathfinder to go take care of business. He knew in his heart that I was a good person and that I wanted to get out of the game. He saw with his own eyes how hard I worked to get out: writing songs, paying for videos and promotional T-shirts. He also knew that the 'hood was ready to get behind the movement. But CZ didn't see this big picture. He was focused on locking a brother up.

I recall one day CZ had just brought my truck back. I had to run up to Parkchester real quick, where Shelly lived at the time, to pick up some money I left in her crib. My man had just given me an offer that I couldn't refuse.

When I got there she was like, "Slow down, what's the

hurry?" I wanted to get in and out fast, but she wanted to go out for dinner. I explained what I had to do, but she complained that I never spent time with her. I told her I'd be right back, but she insisted on going with me. I told her I'd take her to get some food. Once we got on the highway, I thought about that deal I had on the table, and I didn't want to blow the opportunity. "Listen, Shelly, let's go to one of these fast food joints real quick to get something. Then I'll take you back home so I can handle my business."

"Fast food? I'm not going to no fucking McDonald's or White Castle's. Take me out to City Island or somewhere nice. What's so important that you can't take me somewhere nice?"

"Listen, that's none of your business," I said. "Just do this for me this time. Just work with me, Shelly."

Shelly was defiant, saying, "No, I always work with you, it's time for you to work with me. We need to talk."

"I gotta go, so I'll just take you back home." I jumped back on the highway, ready to complete my mission.

"I'm not going home. I am tired of staying in the house all day and night by myself. I don't like this shit anymore," Shelly shouted. "This is not my type of life. Take me downtown to my grandmother's house." This upset me, since I had just come all the way uptown on the highway. I didn't understand why she hadn't asked to go downtown sooner. "Listen, I'm taking you home," I said as I steadily gained more speed.

Shelly began to yell, "No, take me downtown to my grandmother's house *now*, Azie. I'm not playing." She started to swing wildly, hitting me on my arm and head. What the fuck is wrong with this nut? I thought to myself. I ignored her request and kept speeding toward her house.

I woke up in the hospital, surprised to discover a thick brace around my neck! Equally surprising was the realization that I had a wad of money in my pocket. I recalled stashing that money in the glove compartment. What the hell done happened now, I thought.

I rose from my groggy state, hoping my neck wasn't broken. I took the brace off slowly, then I looked in the bathroom mirror. A doctor entered the room and said, "I'm glad you're up. How does your neck feel?" I indicated I was alright as he lightly brushed particles of glass from my head.

"Can you tell me what I'm doing here, doc? And how did all of this money get in my pocket?"

He informed me that I was in a serious car accident. Right then, a cop walked in the room. The look of amazement on his face revealed that he was shocked to see me alive. According to the police officer, my truck spun and flipped across the highway several times before it crashed into a wall. The intensity of the crash caused a wheel to fly right off the axle.

"Your girlfriend flew out the window," said the officer. "She's over there in the other room going crazy. She has a huge hole in her head."

"Can I go see her?"

"Yeah, she's right there in that room. Don't worry, you'll hear her—she's been cursing at everybody since she got here." I went to her room just as the doctors finished stitching her head.

"Are you oka—"

"I told you to take me downtown to my grandmother's house," she angrily interrupted me. Then her head spun completely around without her body moving. She started yelling, "I hate you, I hate you," and started throwing things at me. "All I wanted was for you to take me to dinner. You messed up everything."

I left the room feeling bad. The doctor informed me that she had to stay for X-rays to determine whether her skull was fractured. She sustained a broken leg from the accident and would have to wear a cast for a few months, he said. "She'll be fine. She's just very upset right now. Go home, get some rest, and come back tomorrow. Visiting hours start at nine a.m. Maybe she'll feel a little better then. Right now she doesn't need the stress."

I did visit the next day. She was sitting up in the bed drinking coffee. I walked in the room with some flowers, and put them in the vase. She looked at me as if she was Linda Blair in *The Exorcist*. Suddenly the room got very cold and she said in a strange voice, "It's all your fault, you tried to kill me." She threw her hot coffee on me, and then began yelling for me to get out. "Nurse . . . somebody help me, he's a murderer!"

The doctor came rushing in the room and kindly asked me to leave. They didn't have to do that; I was on my way out anyway.

My next stop was to the junkyard to see my truck.

My Pathfinder looked more like a Jetta; it was totally destroyed. I couldn't figure out how I made it out of that wreck alive. I still didn't know how I got the money from the glove compartment. I didn't have time during the accident to get the money. I must have been tumbling like clothes in a washing machine. I later learned that an honest cop saw the money and put it in my pocket. I thanked God for our lives immediately.

I asked the mechanic what caused the accident. "The front wheel on the driver's side came off. You must have been going a hundred miles an hour," he said.

I asked him, "But how can the front wheel come off of a brand-new car? That doesn't make sense."

"Maybe the bolts weren't tightened properly. Or maybe someone *loosened* the bolts," he replied. "Damn." I thought about CZ. Maybe he wanted to kill me because I knew he was a federal agent.

So in my paranoia, I came up with a crackpot theory. He didn't want to go out like a sucker because I treated him so well. I bought him clothes, and took him under my wing. But he had to do his job. Maybe he felt guilty about turning me over to the law, so he took the sucker route, and tried to kill me in an "accident."

It sounded crazy, but the drug game made people— hustlers, users, and law enforcement agents—do crazy things and get crazy suspicions. But though I wasn't killed, someone was. Shelly never got a chance to tell me that night—she was so emotional because she was a few months pregnant at the time. The accident caused her to lose the baby. She had insisted on going to a restaurant because she wanted to tell me the good news over a nice romantic dinner.

Our tragic loss was my fault. Although I didn't have knowledge of her pregnancy when I drove that night, I still should have driven responsibly because both our lives were precious. It disturbs me to admit that our safety wasn't a priority for me that night. All I could think about was meeting up with this cat to buy a kilo of coke for only $9,000! He stole it from somebody else, which explained the "discount." I drove like a maniac to get those drugs, but they only thing I got was a sore neck and the guilt of destroying an innocent life. Let me tell you: The game is a motherfucker! It loves no one. It's a monster with an insatiable appetite; it even feeds on innocent babies.

On March 13, 1993, Shelly gave birth to my angel Azzia. I believe she arrived right on time to save my soul. It's all about the children. I believe that the same love we have for children is the love God has for us, His children. I just wanted to keep her out of harm's way by any means necessary. The day Azzia was born, New York City was struck with a horrible blizzard. I saw her birth in a symbolic way; she was my guiding light through the vicious storm of life, or as I say, she was my little Rudolph the red-nosed reindeer.

I went through a lot of shit trying to get out of the game and start MobStyle. The game didn't want to let me go under any circumstances. It was like Satan knew I had been talking to God and he didn't want me to have a platform to wake up others.

Our main studio was Funky Slice Studio in Brooklyn.

Two Chinese cats owned it. One was named Dr. B and his man was called Control. They were musicians who played all types of instruments, and they had soul. It seemed like they knew what I wanted; we just clicked. I made some of my best music at Funky Slice: "What's Going on, Black," "Crack the Mack," and "Streetwise." A good studio has to have good clear microphones, no interruptions, and good management. That studio covered all the bases. When it was time to start a session, those cats had everything ready. Our music was set so we could come right in and take care of business. They had an ear for keeping our music real and hardcore. I learned a lot about producing and writing songs from Dr. B and Control.

Studio time cost big money. You might get charged $100 per hour and we might take two or three months to finish an album. But we didn't care how much it cost. We wanted to use music to escape the drug game. Honestly speaking, I probably lost more money than I made from MobStyle. But it was all good because we got to rock shows, meet a lot of good people, make videos, express ourselves, and have fun. I see that our music made other hustlers and the generations after us take the route of rapping over hustling. I believe our group never blew up because of our wicked deeds in the game. I can live with that.

Do I resent the music industry for not putting MobStyle on? Not at all, I leave that for CZ to think about. My resentment toward the music industry is directed at their conspiracy to poison black music with destructive images and lyrics. Industry executives pimp the poor urban experience, then send their kids off to college with the profits. Poor urban kids are brainwashed to be a generation of gangster wannabees and we send them off to prisons and cemeteries.

I must recommend a book to people, especially musicians and recording artists. Sufi Inayat Khan named the book *Music*. He suggests that the science of sound can be used in education, in business, in the industry, in commerce, and in politics in order to bring about a desired result but the best use of it is made in spiritual evolution. By the power of sound or word one can evolve spiritually. Music is the best medium for awakening the soul.

For better or worse, I believe that MobStyle pioneered hustler rap, and gave street cats the opportunity to sell music rather than drugs. Today, many of rap's most popular artists make the leap from drug dealing to music, and we helped to create that, which is something no one can take away from us.

This society poisoned the minds of people with lies and half-truths. I actually helped sell some poison (drugs) myself, but I'm proud of MobStyle. We developed a medicine—through music—that would expose the game and help people see it for what it really was.

Songs like "Crack the Mack," "What's Going On, Black." "Live and Let Die," those songs really helped people in tough circumstances defeat some of their problems. I did not sugarcoat the issues. Many people have approached me—counselors from rehabilitation centers, teachers, students, and even some addicts—and thanked me for making music that spoke to them. Some people told me that a song inspired them to get their life back on the right course.

Although we didn't achieve mainstream success, we did produce three albums: *The Good, the Bad, and the Ugly*, in 1989; *Streetwise* in 1992; and *Game of Death* in 1993.

In 2000, my younger brother Wayne Boogie wanted to keep MobStyle alive, so we added some young, hungry cats with mad flow. We called the group "MS II" (MobStyle 2000). The new members of the group were O-Double, Conrad Shiesty (rest in peace), D-Mack, Kenny Blanco from the Bronx, Wayne Boogie, the young don Corleone, and my nephew Bo (The Nemesis).

We worked hard and finished the album *Blood on My Money* in 2000. We signed a fifty-fifty deal with Artists Only Records, an independent label that had their only distribution route. I felt the tracks were hot but never got their proper airplay. We always had to produce our music independently. We were underground drug dealers who became underground hip-hop artists.

As for me, I knew that music was a good hustle, but if I wanted to keep paper coming in and teach the truth about the drug game, I had to venture off into new hustles.

I deeply believe Rich Porter, Alpo, MobStyle, and I prepared the stage for contemporary rap artists. They make references to us in their songs. This includes Nas, Jay-Z, Jadakiss, and 50 Cent. In his song "There's Been a Murder," Jay-Z refers to himself as Rich Porter's twin brother.

I'm not mad at the rap cats; I have no problem with

seeing another man eat. I just want them to know that others played a very big part in making the rap game so lucrative. Others paved the way for these cats to get rich simply by exercising their freedom of speech.

MobStyle helped make it possible for hustlers to abandon drug dealing and murder. Street cats can use music as their new hustle now. They should show appreciation for this by ridding their music of lyrics that promote their old lifestyle. Put the fun and love back into the music and save the children from having to relive the pain we experienced. Some rap lyrics have put our community into darkness. It's time for us to turn the lights back on "in the building."

Stores that sell this music play a major role in promoting the foolishness. Rappers who have paid their dues and positioned themselves to own their masters have the power to steer their music in a more positive direction.

I wish I could call a meeting, a sort of "last supper" where we could all agree to get this nonsense out of existence. We need to throw all rap promoting bullshit and violence in a pile and burn it, regardless of the money it makes. I would be the first one to do so. I will burn all my compact discs, and ask for anyone who owns any of them to bring them to this last supper ceremony to be symbolically destroyed. This would start a very brave and righteous movement to put our mental and spiritual health before material wealth.

Gangster rap was created in the streets and it will die in the streets. Like it or not, the game is over! I recently saw the movie *Get Rich or Die Trying* about the life of rapper 50 Cent. Right after that, I read a newspaper article discussing the indictment and trial of the heads of rap label Murder Inc.

Both the movie and the Murder Inc. trial clearly show how much the gangster image has shaped the reality of people in the 'hood. Whether the gangsters were real or fictional, we all seem to be fascinated with them: John Gotti, Scarface, Don Corleone, Bugsy Siegel, Lucky Luciano, "Pretty Boy" Floyd, John Dillinger, Al Capone, and Nicky Barnes. We admire them because gangsters break the law and listen to their own authority. They seem to take matters into their own hands. In our ignorance, we emulate these characters and turn into monsters that kill, betray, and maim our own communities.

The *Source* magazine published an issue shouting out all the rap artists behind bars. Prior to reading that article, I didn't know so many artists were incarcerated. I should not have been surprised though. Isn't it strange that rap has almost become synonymous, in some people's minds, with violence and drugs? Isn't it strange that gangster rap—despite the fates of Biggie and Tupac—markets violence and competition to sell music?

Since hip-hop is such a dominant force on the global scene, its influence extends beyond musical boundaries. Some of the most popular video games borrow their characters and style from hip-hop, games like *Grand Theft Auto* and *True Crimes*, for example.

Hip-hop magazines and videos shamelessly exploit sex and violence. Record and magazine executives would not dare have their wives, sisters, or mothers depicted as sex objects, but have no problem depicting other women as whores who will do anything for money. I don't know if life reflects art or art reflects life, but when *I personally viewed some of the most despicable images that have been produced* I thought, "My God, what have we become?"

Rap artists recognize the mentality of their audience, so they give the people what they want or what's popular at the moment. In this way, they are no different from movie writers and directors who recognize that gangster movies bring in big bucks at the box office. Violence, sex, and drugs are sensational to the public, and there's no way around it. To give these movies a taste of authenticity, writers sometimes loosely base their stories on actual people or events.

In the movie *Juice*, the character Bishop, played by Tupac, killed his good friend and later attended his funeral service. He recognized his friend's mother and approached her to give his condolences. "I'm sorry, *Ms. Porter*," he said. To me, the reference to Rich and Donnell's mom was obvious, and I couldn't believe they went there.

The movie *New Jack City*, starring Wesley Snipes and Ice-T, is considered a street classic. The music, the action, and the story were off the hook. I once ate with the writer of that movie, Bill Michael Cooper. He personally told me that he wrote the story loosely based on the lives of Rich, Alpo, and me.

Good or bad, I believe rappers should at least be themselves and represent themselves accurately. It troubles me when cats attempt to emulate another dude's life and claim it as their own. In the 1990s a rapper named Anthony Cruz, who called himself AZ, was a member of the rap clique known as The Firm. Other members included Nas, Nature, and Foxy Brown.

Cruz consistently denies taking my name or imitating my image. If this is true, why did he name his first single "Sugar Hill"? (Especially since he was born in Brooklyn, New York.) The hook for this song was sung by former singer and New York City radio personality Miss Jones. I had the opportunity to speak with her on this matter. I guess someone pulled her coat as to who AZ really was. She came to me with a humble spirit to inquire about the situation and I explained it to her.

"The hook of your song was perfect, but it didn't have the real character playing the role. Azie is my *actual* name, not a nickname I use in music. I was raised in Harlem and grew up in Sugar Hill. A lot of cats followed in our footsteps to provide for their families. I am not mad at you because I understand. I'm not even mad at them. It's alright to have influences, but you should build your own reputation without using another person's name." I think Miss Jones understood my point.

Gangsta rap is not the way, it is in the way. One time I was talking to a woman out of Toronto, Canada, named Lori. She told me about an experiment they were doing at the Botanical Gardens with two identical flowers.

They placed these flowers in separate green rooms and left them alone for twenty-four hours. In one room, soft music played; in the other gangsta rap played. The scientists returned to find only one flower alive. The flower exposed to the gangsta rap died.

Music is a very powerful force; there are musical notes

that can make you happy, sad, excited, or calm. Music consists of sound waves that create specific vibrations in the ear. These vibrations send electrical messages to the brain, stimulating thoughts and emotions.

African-American music forms like the blues, gospel, and jazz are in tune with our nature, full of feeling, spirit, and soul. Even the drums have a soothing, stimulating effect because their rhythmic beat simulates the heartbeat. A baby hears his mother's heartbeat while still in the womb. Some study should be done to determine how sounds influence thought. When we create quality music we create soothing vibrations that promote peace and harmony. We must save our music in order to save our lives.

Now that hip-hop attracts tons of money and unfortunately just as much crime, the law enforcement community is involved. The "hip-hop police" have the rap game under strict surveillance. In fact, a special task force exists just for rappers.

Rap was a door to freedom that was created in the streets. Poor black people created the music form by spinning records and rapping over them. Like anything in its beginning stages, rap had to crawl before it walked. Back in the day, you might be able to enter a party for a dollar or less. Now hip-hop is a multibillion-dollar industry that influences people around the world. A force we created is slowly being lifted from our fingers because we just can't get along without violence. Scott La Rock was killed, along with Tupac, Biggie, Freaky Tah, Big L, Jam Master Jay, and the list goes on.

Too many lives were lost and it makes you really think

and ask, "What's going on, black?" Are we heading the right way? What are we doing wrong? Everything we create starts off good but gets complicated once money is involved: "More money, more problems." I thought the drug game was dirty, but there are more sharks, snakes, and demons in the music industry. People will do anything for money, as I learned the hard way.

I wish I could bring conscious rap artists into the studio to create an album. My dream roster of artists would be off the hook: Erykah Badu, Lauryn Hill, Rakim (the greatest emcee ever), Nas, KRS-One, Chuck D, Mos Def, the cats from Dead Prez, and Common. I'd name the album *Life* and get Dr. Dre to produce it. Powerful minds like that would produce the most creative and powerful hip-hop album ever. I say this with confidence because the artists are real, talented, and passionate.

I notice that many of the most popular rap artists out today used to sell drugs before joining the music industry. I can relate because of my own experiences with Mob-Style. Selling drugs took me from welfare and working in the cleaners to living like I won the lottery. But the shit couldn't last forever.

After almost getting killed I left the game and gave music a try. So I respect cats who leave drug dealing behind to get into music. If you get into rap to escape the drug game and you try to kick truth to free people's minds, I'm with you. If you claim to have stopped selling drugs but use music to still live out your former lifestyle, you're a phony. It's these types of so-called gangsta rappers that I have a problem with.

Game Over

From firsthand experience, I can talk about the hell you go through when you sell drugs: the paranoia, the gold-digging women, the backstabbing brothers, the dirty cops, and the constant threat of violence to yourself or your family. Any truthful hustler will tell you that the money they make is heavenly, but the lifestyle is hell. Most cats get into drug dealing because legitimate avenues of making money are closed to them. Most cats selling drugs have little formal education; most of them, like myself, don't complete high school. Drug dealing is a way for cats to survive. Most dealers work long hours every day of the week to make money, and *most don't make real money.*

Don't believe the hype! Most hustlers do not become rich. In a book named *Freakonomics* by Steven D. Levitt and Stephen J. Dubner, a Chicago street gang was studied. The study showed that the average street-level dealer—the one that makes hand-to-hand sales—only made an average of $3.30 an hour. This is less than minimum wage! Meanwhile, each gang member had a one-in-four chance of being killed.

Yet many of these former hustlers turned rap stars glamorize their drug-dealing days, making it seem like they were kingpins, making millions every year, and murdering anyone who got in their way. If the hustling life was so good to them, why did they leave it to make records? Many of these cats don't want people to know that they left the game because of fear.

Many gangsta rappers leave the drug game and enter the music game, where they don't have to worry about cops or jail. In the music hustle, they can get rich quickly, be famous, and have all the women, just for speaking their minds on an album. In other words, they realized that hip-hop music was the new hustle! That's why you can visit any large black urban community in this country and find people peddling rap CDs and DVDs on the street like crack!

I'm disappointed with most rap artists because they push what the music executives want them to push. When Biggie and Pac left the scene, a void was created in the gangsta rap world. A number of cats stepped up to take their places. This is no coincidence. What gangsta rappers don't know is that they are being used to push a destructive agenda. Racism kills, guns kill, drugs kill, cigarettes kill, alcohol kills, and so-called gangsta rap kills. Real music, however, calms the savage beast.

It's a shame that so-called gangsta rappers kill and assault one another. Why should they have to walk around with bodyguards and bulletproof vests? Many of these rap artists breathe life into subject matter that God put to death long before they arrived. Too many artists admire and praise drug dealers, gangs, and street cliques.

We can begin to understand the mentality of gangster rappers and music executives by observing the names they choose: Gotti, Murder Inc., Bad Boy, Scarface, etc. These are all signs that we are following the wrong path. To be commercially successful, artists want to associate themselves with criminals and thugs. The government sees this and says, "Since you act like criminals and brag about being criminals, we're going to treat you like criminals."

You can't make much money in rap today by telling the

truth; people will call you corny. If you expose the phoniness or foolishness of gangster rappers, you earn the title of playa hater.

Not all rap artists kick negative messages. But righteous hip-hop artists like Dead Prez, KRS-One, Common, and Mos Def don't get the promotions, distribution, or radio play that the gangsta or hustler rappers get. Therefore, they won't sell the huge number of records that the others do.

Imagine if rap artists really spoke on things that mattered. For example, I spit these lyrics on my *Game Over* soundtrack:

I sit at the table of continents
new developments . . . the new-born control the elements
make a wrong decision, a collision
use your third vision
Go astray? You'll find yourself slipping, dipping through
the Milky Way
A moment of silence, let us pray let us pray
A new dimension, first thought listen
A lot of cats wishin' that you don't complete your mission
but up in orbit, our gold we don't sport it
medals of honor? True men go for it
I am HE, follow me
time to open up the mind and find a new galaxy
slow down your speed and you're heading through the polar region

such a quick change of seasons—damn, I'm bleeding
  (Ah-choo!) I'm sneezing
Money is the reason for this treason
You're dipping in and out of spiritual traffic
thoughts bend like plastic—quick, change the graphics
Bullets turn kids to bastards
If it don't bleed, it don't lead
  don't give 'em what they want, give 'em what they need
  *Indeed, I come to feed, if the fruit is rotten, why plant
the seed?*
  Use your brain, Clark Kent and Lois Lane
  forecast cloudy: it looks like rain
  up here . . . no window wipers
  *The force protects the viper to keep the nonsense out my
cipher . . .*

Another cut from the CD I like goes like this:

360 degrees completes a circle
365 (off balance) makes me wanna hurt you
It's sad, yo, "The Color Purple" got us living virtue
Bill Gates, enemy of the state
up top stop—don't playa hate, about face
up ahead, frozen lakes
wait—navigate
I loved the game, I loved to ball
I been there, I done that, I swear I had it all
respond to a higher call
Old mind die, young stay alive

new common law rise!
Free enterprise
Illumince, illuminati, Mayor Giuliani, lil' John Gotti's
hotties
Knock it off, become God-bodies
Play to win, fuck the top ten
Seize the trees, breathe again, oxygen
It's time, so let it begin
See, the game plain destroys man
black it out, go back hand-to-hand but overstand
Interact, react, jump back, THEN attack
then escalade parade your Benz truck Cadillac
Let it render, G-O-D #1 contender
1-2-6 Peace! Return to sender. . . .

I believe we need lyrics like this that force us to think about where we are and where we need to be. Lyrics can still be clever and use slick words, but they should be clever and slick for God, not for death and destruction.

There's been a lot of talk about getting the rap community involved in politics. There are some artists who might make good politicians, but this society would never allow them to be. The powers that be would hand-pick rap artists who kick the messages they want them to kick—not the truth.

These rap politicians would be used to pacify us, to make us think everything is alright. Honestly speaking, these politicians would be controlled behind the scenes like puppets. Many black politicians are controlled in this exact way right now. Money controls everything in this world and most of the politicians, just like drug dealers and everybody else, are on a paper chase for money. You either go with the powers that be, or you go against them. Those who support them are paid well. Those who resist them are eliminated one way or the other.

So I don't think that rap politicians will really help. If the rappers want to help us, they have to do it by creating a musical ministry that teaches, heals, and empowers the listeners. They have to stop glorifying death, and they must begin to keep it real in the truest sense. The main campaign we need in the 'hood right now is a campaign to expose and reject rappers with messages of death, destruction, and foolishness. Everybody in our community should be encouraged to stop supporting such rap artists. If we stop buying trash, the artists will stop making it!

The eighties were the golden era of hip-hop. Every block had rap crews that battled each other for bragging rights. Sometimes opposing crews contained family members or good friends. When people battled back then, it was business, not personal. I don't remember anybody getting shot or attacked as a result of a battle.

If someone told me back then that one day, emcees would get killed over words they said on records, I wouldn't believe it. The tragic murders of Biggie and Tupac showed me that things had changed for the worse in the rap game.

Today hip-hop is a multibillion-dollar industry that has strongly influenced fashion, athletics, and public relations throughout the world. Hip-hop has turned out to be a successful adult. In its infant stage, however, hip-hop wasn't rich or glamorous. Whites and Asians didn't accept it yet. Its main contribution was that it gave poor black youth a platform to express themselves and to get props while doing so.

Harlem to Hollyhood

14

After all I had been through I felt I had a very powerful story to share with the world. My experiences with MobStyle made me familiar with filming music videos. I wanted to enter the world of moviemaking.

I got a sign that it was time to move in this direction while I was at Shelly's crib one night. I stayed up all night thinking about my future, and fell asleep on her couch. I had a dream that I was in a movie theater watching a movie about my life. I woke up but couldn't go back to sleep, so I walked outside for some fresh air.

Bright lights and a big truck across the street caught my attention. They were filming a movie, so I went over to investigate. I asked one of the guys on the set if he knew the name of the movie and he said "Sugar Hill." He told me to go by the gate because Wesley Snipes was over there.

Maybe this was the meaning of my dream, I thought. That night I decided to write a screenplay about my life.

I felt our youth needed to hear the truth in a language they could understand. It's like Rich, Alpo, and I were the shepherds and a lot of sheep in the 'hood blindly followed us into the wicked side of life. I knew that anyone following our example would be led to the slaughter. Our jewelry, cars, women, and power hypnotized people. I know this for a fact because of the way people followed us around, and the way young cats looked at us with admiration. This was a case of the blind leading the blind.

Few people were close enough to know what we had to do behind the scenes to floss the way we did. My shooting, along with the deaths of Rich and his brother Donnell pulled the beautiful mask off of the drug game and showed the ugly scars and bruises it had underneath. I wanted everybody to know how ugly the drug game was. To me, it was personal. I lost too many friends to the streets, and damn near lost my own life.

Many brothers and sisters in the 'hood cannot read, and many of those who can choose not to. However, we do watch movies. In fact, I once read a statistic that said African Americans account for 70 percent of the movie tickets sold in America, even though we only represent 12–15 percent of the United States population. Black people go to the movies religiously and like sponges, absorb much of what Hollywood shows us. I wanted to use a movie to reach the minds and hearts of the youth. Basically, I felt a movie about my experiences would be a strong public service announcement against life in the drug game.

The movie about Rich, Alpo, and me was later titled *Paid in Full*, but I originally titled the screenplay *Trapped*. This word best described how I felt in the drug game. That's how most cats in the 'hood feel. The whole goal of creating a ghetto is to trap its residents, to cut them off from the resources and information they need to be strong.

Just about everything good is scarce in America's ghettos, while everything bad is provided in abundance. The average ghetto resident in America has easier access to guns and drugs than they do to quality education and employment. Being poor, uneducated, and unsafe creates a situation where you have no real power or freedom. You *feel* trapped, and in some ways you *are* trapped.

Malcolm X, speaking at a Harlem rally in the sixties, explained the forces that led people into lives of crime. He said that miseducation, low self-esteem, and lack of employment and job skills made our people feel trapped in an endless cycle of despair and hopelessness. Because we saw no way out of our misery, he explained, we turned to weed, alcohol, heroin, and cocaine, seeking artificial relief from our pain. Although Malcolm gave the speech at least twenty years before my entry into the drug game, his analysis was completely accurate. When I read his autobiography and realized that he named one chapter "Trapped," I knew I'd found the perfect title for my screenplay.

I started writing the screenplay in 1993, but many obstacles delayed my progress. For one, I wasn't trained to write screenplays. I did have some experience with creating the script for videos, but a screenplay required a certain format and the ability to write strong dialogue. Also, I wasn't familiar with how things worked in the movie industry. I didn't know how to get my ideas to the people who could bring my story to life on the screen.

I ran into a young brother named Austin Phillips who'd just finished film school and was eager to work on my project. We hooked up and eventually wrote a 189-page screenplay. I still believe that original screenplay could have become a three-hour epic along the lines of *Scarface* or *The Godfather*.

We met with lawyers and agents who all told us no one would touch the project. We also learned that our script was too long. Each page of script equals one movie minute. The unedited version of *Trapped* would have been a three-hour-and-fifteen-minute movie.

By 1996, Austin and I were satisfied with our product, and began shopping it around to get a movie deal. I worked with some Russian cats down on Wall Street for about a year. They seemed interested in my project, and agreed to finance the movie.

The deal fell through when I began to feel they were dragging their feet; no real progress was made. I later heard that the feds shut down their offices.

The project seemed to be going nowhere until I ran into a brother I knew named Shep. He had a connection at Roc-A-Fella Records, he said, and Damon Dash wanted to get involved with my movie. We set up a meeting, and I pitched the story to Dame.

"Me, Rich, and 'Po were getting mad money real young.

We was ahead of our time," I said. "We bought jewelry, cars, and houses like most people bought socks. We had love in the 'hood and we helped other people to eat. Even you music industry cats starting copying our style and shouting us out in your songs. We were like the young shepherds of the 'hood, but we steered the youth in the wrong direction. We got cats hustlin' and flossin' like we did, and that shit has to stop, 'cause it's killing the 'hood. This movie *Trapped* speaks in the language youth understand, and it will bring them to the light."

"I respect where you're comin' from," Dame said. "We both from Harlem, and we need to work together to show people where all this shit came from. I'm telling you, once we get behind this movie, it's gonna be larger than life! Trust me, you won't have to worry about money at all," he said.

I made the decision to work with Damon Dash. He seemed to be interested in my project, and I was anxious to get the movie done. This began a five-year business relationship with Roc- A-Fella Films.

I didn't necessarily believe all Dame's talk about giving Harlem props or making me rich. I made a transition from hustling to movies, and some of the shit was flat-out new to me. But some things exist in any profession, like telling people what you want them to hear. I wasn't a movie executive, but I knew enough to know that Dame had his own interests, namely himself and Cam'Ron.

Dash figured my movie would put the film division of his record company on the map. The rap artist Cam'Ron was Dame's childhood friend. Dame probably saw the movie as a vehicle to promote his man. I didn't let these issues faze me, first of all because everybody has self-interests; people always approach things from the standpoint of how it will benefit them. Secondly, I had my own agenda. No amount of money could resurrect the dead, but I did want to ensure their families were comfortable financially. I wanted some of the movie's proceeds to go to Rich Porter's family and the families of the people killed in my drug factory in 1987.

Roc-A-Fella Records' star artist and executive Jay-Z was present at some of the meetings, but it was clear that Jigga was more of a behind-the-scenes force in the movie. Dame did most of the talking and negotiating.

Once we completed the necessary paperwork, Dame had me work with a number of writers. First, they brought the brother who wrote *New Jack City*. I didn't like his writing or his approach to the project.

A young Russian cat named Mat Zeronick came on board, but his writing was weak too. Dame assembled a host of talented writers, but my story and my street background scared them off. I began thinking that something deeper was going on—something deeper then Dame Dash or Jay-Z. If Dame and Jay say they are from the streets, why would they want to rewrite a street masterpiece written by a brother who knew the streets firsthand? I didn't understand.

I discussed this with my homeboy and he reminded me that record and movie industry cats couldn't get in such powerful positions without working for larger powers and interests.

"The record and movie industries are nothing but mind control, brother," he warned me. "Brother Malcolm said long ago that popular black people are used to promote the agenda of other people. Do the math." He went on to tell me that the youth were like sheep in that they quickly followed the plan laid out before them. "You better be careful before you wind up like Biggie and Tupac," he warned. "There is a conspiracy to destroy our minds with spiritual warfare," he added.

"Are you saying my life is in danger?" I asked.

"Yes! Jesus was crucified because he spoke truth to wake up the people. To prevent him from coming back and to make people forget about his message, they buried him in a cave and placed a huge rock in front. They use these movies and songs to spread lies and deception so they can kill the spirit of the people. If they see you have all this energy and that the people feel you, they want to take that energy and use it for their own purposes."

His logic was strong and he had my full attention. It was part sermon and part history lesson. "Come on, brother," he continued, "don't you ever believe that they will let some black drug dealer walk in off the street and tell them what to do. It may seem like these rap artists are running things, but don't get it twisted. They deal in deception. Don't ever forget that the first slave ship they packed us on was named *Jesus*.

"We are a sleeping giant and they know astrologically that it is time for us to wake up and start loving each other the way God planned it. For some reason your story threatens certain people. Your story deals with the spirit.

Don't blow it, Azie, we need you. They will use anything in their power, including money, to keep us asleep. But remember: There is no money in heaven, no bribes, no payoffs. We must operate in the mind of God. Just fall back and let the Most High handle His business. Forget about the money; it's time to save your soul. Look at the names: Roc-A-Fella, Cluminatti, State Property, Diplomats—you tell me where MobStyle and *Trapped* fit in?"

Eventually they found a screenwriter named Thulani Davis and a director named Chuck Stone to work on the movie. (People might be familiar with Chuck's famous "What's up" Budweiser commercials.) They were both talented, but they brought a different perspective to my project. I guess this always occurs when you collaborate with someone else, but I was really disappointed with their vision for the movie.

When I first met with Roc-A-Fella, I was excited and hopeful. Imagine the pride I felt that someone was doing a movie about my life. How many people get to make a film about themselves, or to see one made about them while they're still alive? But after dozens of meetings with the movie representatives, my feelings changed. I felt like someone took my life, commercialized it, and stripped it of all the truth and power it formerly contained.

In 1996, Roc-A-Fella Films changed the movie title from *Trapped* to *Paid in Full*. My title emphasized struggle, danger, and a sense of urgency. The new title emphasized money. The title was not the only thing that changed in the editing room. What began as a story of transformation, and an indictment against dirty cops, lawyers, and lawmakers, became another watered-down ghetto flick. Five years and fifteen rewrites later, the finished product looked very little like the movie I wrote. I guess that's what happens when you go from Harlem to Hollyhood.

They did manage to keep some of my ideas, like the character's names. The character representing me was called "Ace," meaning "The One." Rich's little brother, Donnell, was named "Sunny," which represented warmth, life, and truth. Donnell's uncle—who eventually had Donnell kidnapped and murdered—was named "Ice." His name represented my perception of Donnell's uncle: cold and ruthless.

My frustration over Roc-A-Fella's vision for the movie made me stay away from the set during the movie's production. However, I did get to meet some of the actors. Mekhi Phifer portrayed Rich Porter's character in the movie. Mekhi gave strong performances in a number of films like *Clockers* and *Soul Food*, and on the TV show *ER*. A Harlem brother like myself, Phifer was a young, cool, level-headed cat.

Wood Harris played my character in the movie. People might remember him as the outspoken black linebacker in the film *Remember the Titans* with Denzel Washington. He is also known for playing the character of Avon Barksdale in the popular HBO series *The Wire*. Avon Barksdale's character is a drug kingpin in Baltimore, Maryland. Harris also played the great Jimi Hendrix in *The Jimi Hendrix Story* that aired on HBO.

Wood hung out with me for a few days and seemed sincerely interested about portraying me accurately. I felt he did a pretty good job, and many people who know me commented on his ability to represent my laid-back style.

I never chilled with Cam'Ron too much, but I must say he portrayed Alpo well. He gave an award-worthy performance.

Miramax Films released *Paid in Full* in October of 2002, eight years after I began writing the screenplay. Box office sales were terrible; the film grossed a total of $3 million. Some movies make up to ten times that figure in the first weekend of their release. Some movies make more than $3 million during the first *day* of their release.

So what did the poor box office numbers mean? Was the movie wack? Was it that people did not feel the story? People have their own opinions, but I believe the movie performed poorly because of poor support. *Paid in Full* was only shown in 236 theaters throughout the United States. Contrast this with Eminem's movie *8 Mile*, which played in 2,646 theaters.

Not only did the public have little access to go see the movie, very few people knew about it. There were no mega-size billboards advertising the movie. No ads that I can recall were placed with leading magazines, or aired on radio stations. The movie had weak promotion and distribution. Furthermore, street cats bootlegged the movie several months before it was released! Despite all of this, the DVD version of the movie has sold well over a million copies. The bottom line is that people will go out and buy or rent a story that really speaks to them.

As for all the money Dame promised me? Let's keep it real. I received a total of $100,000 for my story, my writing, and my consultation. I would have been cool with at least getting that money in a lump sum. But the $100,000 I received was over the course of six years! I received no royalties or residuals, yet others made millions from my life and ideas.

What upset me more than the money issue was how my original story was watered down. My original screenplay, *Trapped*, addressed key issues and transformations in my life. It also explored the complexity of life as a hustler.

Paid in Full fell short in these areas. For example, the finished product made little reference to the social forces that push so many youth to sell and use drugs. My experiences in school and decision to drop out were not mentioned. There was no portrayal of corrupt law enforcement officials and how they cooperate with drug dealers and other criminals just to make a fast buck. And what about how the movie portrayed me? Based on viewing the movie, some people think I snitched on Alpo!

Paid in Full shows that I left the drug game after my shooting, but fails to show how I changed my life. No one watching the film sees all the reading I did or all the visits I made to churches, mosques, and synagogues. Movie audiences saw no evidence that I created a rap group named MobStyle. The movie leaves people thinking that my character betrayed a fellow partner in crime. Alpo, who caused a lot of death and destruction, is glamorized and portrayed as some sort of street hero.

Instead of promoting my opinion that the drug game is over, *Paid in Full* encourages people to idolize the game and its star players. A movie has once again poisoned the minds of our youth by distorting the truth. Hollywood has always had an agenda to feed us negative images to keep us ignorant and controllable. What makes this worse today is that we have a ton of so-called music industry thugs who seek wealth and fame by pimping ghetto pain and tragedy.

If I could go back in time I would maintain more editorial control over the film. I would hire older, more seasoned people to direct and produce the movie. Last but not least, I would hire the best legal representation I could get to negotiate the best financial deal for myself.

My original screenplay, *Trapped*, was revised and rewritten over fifteen times; the movie *Paid in Full* that evolved from my screenplay was a Hollywood production. It simply strayed far away from the truth. I realized that I had to create a project that I had complete control over. I decided to shoot a documentary showing actual people and places that were important in my life.

A brother named Troy Reed and I began filming a documentary about my life called *Game Over* in 1999. His company is called Street Stars Inc. Troy is like the Spike Lee of street docudramas. He produced stories about Larry Davis, Guy Fisher and Nicky Barnes, and Carlton Hines. Troy has released a number of documentaries about black urban legends involved in crime, and I encourage people to check them out. If nothing else, these true stories will help you understand the causes and consequences of inner-city crime from the hustler's point of view. These documentaries should be required viewing in high schools throughout this country.

Harlem to Hollyhood

We scheduled *Game Over*'s release for 2001, but it was bootlegged so crazy in the streets that we had to speed up the release date to 2000. I don't have exact figures on the sales of the documentary, but I know Troy produced and sold over 150,000 units initially. When you add up all the bootleg copies sold by street vendors, the documentary clearly sold out of this world.

Later, Troy created another edition of the documentary and got rap artist Jadakiss to narrate the new version. I know for a fact that *Game Over* is known in Atlanta, Boston, D.C., and Detroit. Once one person views it, they recommend it to someone else. Word of mouth throughout the streets helped sell the documentary without major corporate promotion and distribution.

The highlight of working on the documentary was getting Patricia Porter involved in the project. Pat needed to be part of the project for two reasons. First of all, she needed to vent. The tragedies Pat experienced are almost impossible to believe. Both her brothers were killed, I was almost killed, and her father was struck by a car and killed while crossing the street. These circumstances might have caused the average woman to kill herself or someone else. But Pat managed to move on to lead a productive life. In my opinion, she is the strongest person I know, and she deserves everything good that comes to her. Roc-A-Fella and Miramax Film companies should adequately compensate Pat.

The second reason Pat needed to be in my documentary concerned the famous *F.E.D.S* magazine article about myself, Rich, and Alpo. *F.E.D.S.* is a magazine that features stories about street hustlers and urban crime. Many of its biggest supporters are on lockdown in this country's prisons. In the late 1990s, *F.E.D.S.* magazine interviewed me. They wanted me to reflect on the drug game and my role in it.

That was the first issue of *F.E.D.S.* and I'm sure my article helped the magazine sell like hotcakes. As we all know, magazines use controversy to sell. The next thing I know, *F.E.D.S.* released an issue in which Alpo granted an exclusive interview from prison. He wanted to tell his side of the story, which was only right.

He admitted killing Rich and explained the purpose behind it, which took courage. Although 'Po expressed remorse for killing Rich, he made allegations about Rich that made him seem shady. Pat read both interviews; she heard my side of the story and Alpo's. Neither Rich nor Donnell were alive to join the discussion. So Pat wisely used the documentary to represent the memory of her slain brothers.

Anyone who saw *Game Over* will admit that Pat did a hell of a job. It was obviously difficult for her to recall those painful memories, and many times she had to fight back tears as she spoke. But she refused to let her pain get in the way of speaking the truth. Anybody can be strong when things go well. Only champs can be strong and hold it together when the shit hits the fan. Her poise and strength under fire give her status in my heart that no one else will ever have. I have nothing but love and respect for Pat.

The beginning of *Game Over* focuses on me, Rich, and Alpo. Viewers begin to understand our personalities, and they get a sense of our flashy lifestyles. However, I did not want my documentary to glamorize the cars, money, and women. I deliberately used most of the documentary to discuss my shooting, and the deaths of Rich and Donnell.

The documentary featured news coverage discussing my attack and newspaper headlines that captured the story. I showed an excerpt of a courtroom scene where one of my shooters addresses the court. The cat curses out people in the courtroom, then defiantly demands that the judge sentence him and let him go. I wanted people to see how cold and deadly the drug game is.

I wanted to put a face to the people killed, so they wouldn't be anonymous victims. I showed several pictures of Rich and Donnell, including newspaper headlines and clips about Donnell's abduction.

Perhaps the saddest part of *Game Over* is a clip from what would have been Donnell's eighth-grade graduation. The principal is shown calling out students' names as they come up to receive their certificates. After he reads Donnell Porter's name, he informs the crowd that in light of Donnell's tragic death, his sister, Patricia, would receive his certificate. You can't help but feel the pain when Pat slowly walks up to the podium, receives Donnell's certificate, and exits the stage with her head down.

Game Over was very successful thanks in large part to Pat. Toward the end of the documentary, Pat warns young brothers about getting involved in a game where there are no real friends, no real love, and no real honor. She goes on to warn young ladies about getting involved with drug dealers. She sadly explains how she had minks, furs, diamonds, cars, and other material things, but how none of those things could bring her brothers back to life.

I felt very honored when the anti-drug component of Russell Simmons's Hip-Hop Summit Action Network was named "Game Over" in tribute to my documentary. If we have helped anyone to leave or never get involved with the drug game, then maybe, just maybe . . . I've earned my wings.

15
Blind, But Now I See

My life involved lots of good, bad, and ugly experiences. Sharing the details in this book has helped me to reflect on my life and the lessons I've learned. I think every person should take some time to do this; this process helps us grow and mature.

I already explained how I stood out from other hustlers in my day, and how I took pride in customizing my cars and jewelry. There are so many things for which I am fortunate. In a world where most people jump on the bandwagon, or follow trends, I've always been a leader.

Another quality that helped me through the years is that I respected everyone's boundaries. When I hustled, I did not try to control another dealer's territory. I respected how they got down as long as they respected my operation.

People who know me well say I'm lucky. They say that

because things I get involved with tend to be successful. But to keep it real, luck has nothing to do with it. What people call "luck" I call "God." God has always held my hand, and spoken to me throughout my life. I also had good intuition, a good ability to read people and situations. Good fortune comes from God, but also the individual. I was never a selfish dude chasing dollars and stepping over everybody in the process. In the streets, my motto was always "Eat and let eat." If everybody eats, then everybody is happy. Who has time to be jealous?

The quality that has kept me alive through all the shit I've been through is discretion. Other brothers in the game were arrogant and vain. It wasn't enough that they made tons of money. They had to show everybody in the 'hood how wealthy they were. Brothers had to rock the latest clothes, sneakers, expensive jewelry, hot cars, etc. Cats had to drive their convertibles with the top down, blasting music for the world to hear. It was their way of saying, "Look at me, I'm important. I'm the man!"

Other hustlers attended every party they could, not to have fun and meet people, but to have a public stage to show off. Back in the eighties, you could find major street hustlers profiling at clubs like the Rooftop and the S&S club in Harlem. I was the complete opposite. I stayed away from the clubs and the parties. I dressed down. I didn't want my name in the streets. I rarely took pictures with other hustlers. The less you knew about Azie, the better. I didn't compete with people for the spotlight; I let them have it. I didn't want a deejay to shout me out at a summer jam. I didn't need to be recognized or acknowledged. This ability to lay low helped me stay under the radar of street niggas and the law. I believe it helps to explain how I survived.

Nowadays, I understand that people who do things to get attention are basically insecure. They don't feel special or valuable, because their self-worth comes from the outside. They need to get props and praise from other people. True respect starts on the inside and works its way out. True respect comes from knowing that you are special whether you wear Nikes or Payless sneakers.

I truly believe that insecurity, vanity, and arrogance are the key reasons that people create enemies. This may sound weird, but many times the people who talk the loudest, boast the most, and demand the spotlight are people who have some serious self-esteem and self-love issues.

Part of reviewing the past is to learn from mistakes. The one quality that hurt me in the past was my tendency to trust people too much. I'm starting to learn now that it's hard to trust anyone. This bad habit comes from thinking that people share my values and get down like I do. I think about how I wrote the screenplay about my life called *Trapped*, and how I trusted Damon Dash to develop it.

Everybody wants to live a comfortable life: we all want to live well. I would be lying to say it wasn't hard to adjust when I left the game. Certain friends and family members turned their backs on me when I stopped bringing in big dough. I no longer had all the gadgets, cars, and other luxuries.

Game Over

I would try to convince brothers to leave the game, and cats would think, "That nigga Azie is out his fucking mind!" I felt isolated from everybody. But for the first time in a long time, I was able to get a good night's sleep. I wasn't looking over my shoulder every fifteen minutes. I didn't have to think about who was trying to set me up or sell me out. For the first time in a long time, I was at peace; there were no more sleepless nights.

"Where's all that shit he used to have?"

"That nigga ain't flossing no more!"

These are the thoughts I'm sure many people have about me. I don't miss the money. What I do miss is all my homies who died in the drug game.

Some people suspect I have some hidden stash of money somewhere. Others think I have one hundred cars parked in some mystery garage. I guess they want to breathe life into the drug game and keep the legend alive. Personally, I want to kill the legend of Azie. The drug game needs no mouth-to-mouth resuscitation, it needs to be murdered, once and for all. So I'm proud to say that anything I have now, I obtained legitimately.

My near-death experience made me do some soul searching. My antennas went up, and my mind began to pick up ideas on a whole other frequency. I realized that the money, jewelry, and cars were all *temporary*. Once I embraced the truth about the direction of my life, I began to have a spiritual battle inside. The little voice inside tried to pull me up the spiritual ladder. I tried to climb this ladder, but I was so used to living in the flesh and dealing in the game. As a result, it was very difficult to just walk away from the game cold turkey. Cats constantly approached me about getting back into the game and I did come out of "retirement" a few times.

Listening to the voice of God forced me to see things I didn't want to deal with. I lost the love I had for the drug game. I began to love knowledge; the more I learned, the more I wanted to learn.

The mind is an incredible piece of work. Once your mind is right, things fall into place. You attract the right people, ideas, and experiences into your world. Having the right frame of mind in the early nineties led me to view Spike Lee's movie *Malcolm X*. Just like the movie *Scarface* got me hyped about entering the drug game, this movie got me hyped about leaving it alone.

I was so impressed with the movie that I decided to read Malcolm's autobiography. The next thing you know, an old friend let me borrow some tapes of brother Malcolm's speeches. The more I read and heard about Malcolm X, the more I saw my own story. Like Malcolm, I grew up in an environment with few resources and support. I also dropped out of school early, and got caught up in the drug game. A tragic event happened to Malcolm that set him on the right path; I had the same experience. I felt that if Malcolm could come from the bottom and educate himself to think right and do right, so could I.

I remember watching the movie *Panthers*, about the Black Panther Party for Self Defense, founded by Bobby Seale and Huey P. Newton. The movie showed how the Panther organization was destroyed. There was a scene where some government agents presented this young brother with drugs and encouraged him to distribute them throughout his community.

First they destroyed the leadership, and then they used drugs to put the community to sleep. Once the community was drugged up, the struggle for equality, justice, and freedom was put on the back burner. Instead of fighting for freedom, people were fighting to get high. This film made me realize that like the brother in the movie, I was nothing more than a fool used to dope up the 'hood. When I made the connections, and put two and two together, I felt ashamed for having been so ignorant. I hated the role I played in the destruction of my community.

This is when I started to turn down the volume in my life and get serious. For two years, I went into exile to get my mind right. Nobody heard from me during this time—my friends, former business partners, not even my own mother. I needed time to myself without all the distractions and bullshit in my life.

My first stop was at a Christian bookstore where I purchased a movie called *Jesus of Nazareth*. In fact, biblical and political movies became my favorite form of entertainment. The movie *JFK*, about the assassination of President John F. Kennedy, blew my mind. I remember thinking, "Damn, this government is crooked!"

Of course, government corruption wasn't new to me. I remembered all the corrupt cops, lawyers, and judges during my hustling days. I remembered how lawyers took my case (and my money) even though they *knew* I was guilty. Then there were the cops who would bust me with drugs, take fistfuls of money, and let me keep the coke!

However, the corruption I witnessed in the drug game was on a small scale compared to the corruption taking place at the highest levels of government. This corruption, I later found out, did not stop at the presidential level. After all, the president is only the mouthpiece, or spokesperson. The real power lies with the bankers, businessmen, and military establishment. They use the politicians to legitimize their actions. It seemed like one movie or book led me to another.

When you get put on to new information, you might think you are the only one who knows about it. Street-corner conversations with brothers more knowledgeable than I made it clear that I had a lot to learn and unlearn. People suggested further sources for me to research and I did. Tapes by David Ike and books like *The Greatest Secret* and *Behold a Pale Horse* opened my mind.

Foul play, I learned, extended way beyond Harlem, the White House, or a few dirty politicians. Various secret societies use their money and political influence to dominate the entire world. Politicians, supported by bankers, create wars to control three things: land, money, and our minds!

Books and tapes gave me important information, but I needed more. I wanted more than facts and dates; I wanted to find a community of people that shared my views and values. Since I wanted to stay on the righteous path, I started visiting different houses of God. Inspired by brother Malcolm X, I went to a Nation of Islam mosque.

The sermons were powerful and full of energy, but the sermons weren't the most impressive feature of the mosque. What really got my attention were the people.

The men stood straight and tall, and they walked with authority. The women had the most beautiful complexions I'd ever seen. Their skin seemed to glow! Their eyes were bright, and their smiles were warm and friendly. I also visited the Jehovah Witnesses' Kingdom Hall meetings and a few Baptist churches.

My experiences in these different houses of God were mostly positive. However, I couldn't help thinking that religions are so divided. They all seemed more interested in rigidly defending *their* beliefs and *their* will. I don't consider myself "holy" and I'm definitely no prophet. But I have strong feelings about spirituality. As I see it, God's people are those who understand His laws and do His will. God's people come from all races and religious backgrounds.

Instead of embracing each other in a spirit of unity, we maintain divisions in the name of religion. For example, try to hold a meeting with a mixed group of Muslims, Jews, Christians, etc. Within fifteen minutes, they would begin arguing about what God's proper name is, the proper way to worship Him, and so on. God is too powerful and wise to concern Himself with our arrogance and pettiness.

Denominations, political parties, or gang affiliations may matter to us, but I refuse to believe the Supreme Being recognizes any of it. Personally, I don't follow a certain religion, because religion consists of manmade laws. I try to follow God's law.

We can understand God's nature by using our minds to observe things around us. I believe the sun is God. The sun provides everything we need for life: fruits, vegetables, rain, warmth, etc. The ancient Egyptian Pharaoh

Akhenaten created a movement that viewed God as the sun. The original people of the Earth prayed to the sun, because the sun was responsible for their crops. Therefore, what I'm saying is not new or crazy.

Part of the reason mankind is so messed up is because we base our lives on the moon rather than the sun. In Genesis 1:16 we learn: "And God made two great lights; the greater light to rule the day, and the lesser light to rule the night: he made the stars also."

Just as the Earth revolves around the sun, all living things on Earth are supposed to revolve around the sun. When does a new day begin? In this culture, a new day starts at midnight. How can a new day start in the dark? Day should begin when the sun rises. Instead, we revolve around the moon.

People teach that Jesus was the Son of God, who was sent to wash our sins away and save us. How does one man save an entire planet? God sent many great people during different times to educate and enlighten His people: Gandhi, Bob Marley, Malcolm X, Martin Luther King, Jr., and the list goes on. Jesus really represents the type of character and qualities we should have if we follow God's laws.

Religious people also teach the concept of heaven and hell. I don't believe in a place called hell. I believe that after we die, our spirits will go back to the sun. God will not have some judgment day when He looks up everything you ever did and rewards or punishes you accordingly.

Upon death, all people—regardless of their wickedness

or righteousness—will return to their source, the sun. Man developed the ideas of heaven and hell to persuade followers to do God's will. If you obey, you live in paradise, and if you disobey, you receive eternal punishment. This is the same way parents discipline their children: rewards and punishments. This approach might work for humans, but does this sound like the reasoning of an almighty God to you?

"Hell," if you want to call it that, exists right here on Earth. Living on a wicked frequency will cause you pain in the form of lost friendships, disease, murder, and failure. And that pain will be eternal, unless you change your ways and begin living in the light. God is a God of grace, forgiveness, and hope, not a God of destruction and limitation.

We've also been taught that hell is hot. I see things differently. I believe hell is cold. In fact, I believe hell is frozen—not a frozen place, but a frozen attitude. When something freezes, it is dead and motionless. Hell represents a situation and a state of mind that is negative, dead, and non-productive.

Like religion, race is a meaningful concept that is often misused. I'm not one of those people who say "I have no race." Racially speaking, I identify myself as a black man, and anyone who sees me would do the same. To me, it's a useful way of classifying people. The problem with race is that people use it to rank your intelligence and character. Quick judgments get made about your sex drive, your intelligence, and your honesty, all based on the amount of skin pigment you have.

Once we use race to judge other people or blame them

for our problems, then race goes against cosmic law. "The white man made me rob, steal, or cheat." When will that same ole conversation end? Let's keep it real. White society created situations that make life hard for black people. They enslaved our forefathers, and prevented us from getting a solid education or a decent job. This is all true. But do we as black people take any responsibility for our own problems? Rich's death, Donnell's death, Charlie's death, and my aunt's death were at the hands of black people. White society made cocaine available to me, but I chose to sell it. It's not about black or white; it's about wrong or right.

Confining ourselves to race will deprive us of many opportunities to learn and grow. As a child, I remember people always teasing black kids who dressed differently, spoke differently, or listened to "white" music. If you did well in school or played an instrument, you were "trying to be white." Many youth grow up feeling ashamed to be themselves for fear of being labeled "white." What message does this send? Do we really believe that people can't be proud of their race and also expose themselves to different things?

I listen to music and speeches by all types of people; my only concern is that they speak truth and enhance my mind. I have found that there are many people today of different races who know the truth and attempt to teach the truth to all who will listen. If you don't believe me, listen to "white boys" like Dave Matthews, Peter Gabriel, Phil Collins, and Pink Floyd. They sing songs on a spiritual plane. Cats who dismiss them just because they're white are ignorant. Throughout time, God has sent many messengers and prophets to enlighten the world. Those messengers may come in any form.

Race is important mostly because society has made it important. Being proud of your heritage and fighting for equality is good. But race isn't the only way of understanding the world. Life is a skyscraper, and too many black people will only get to the fourth floor if they limit themselves to the racial plane. If we train ourselves to recognize truth, and not race, we'll be all right.

Everyone wants to know what I'm up to these days. "How does Azie pay his bills?" "What does he live on?" One thing no one has to ever worry about is how Azie will make money. I know how to make money. If you drop me off anywhere in the world, I'll make a way for myself. I always made money, money never made me.

Another question everyone wants to ask is whether I still have cars, jewelry, or money left over from my hustling days. I used to have a phone watch that included a phone book. In that phone book, I had the names and numbers of people who owed me money. All together, the streets owed me about $475,000. I had about three or four cars at the time, which added up to another $200,000, and the house in Long Island, which was valued at about $190,000. My bills at the time were easily $9,000 per month. Yet I never went to collect the money that cats owed me. I left the drug game and everything associated with it.

When I left the game alone, my situation improved in more ways than one. When you bag huge amounts of coke, you actually wind up inhaling the dust. There's no way around this, so all those years I bagged coke, I was probably getting a contact high. When I stopped dealing, my energy level increased, my complexion cleared up, and I felt healthy again. The nightmares I had during my hustling years stopped, and I began to have beautiful dreams again. I wanted to feel like that all the time, so I made the choice to save my life. I did go back to selling a few times, but when I decided to stop for good, I didn't look back.

To recognize truth, we have to observe the signs and symbols around us. I believe God uses symbols to let us know we are on the right path. An important symbol in my life is the number 126. I find different combinations of the numbers in just about every area of my life.

- I'll begin with my first name, Azie—AZ. A is the first letter of the alphabet, while Z is the twenty-sixth.
- After the fire in the Bronx we moved to Harlem. Our address was 723 Saint Nicholas Avenue, apartment number 6. 7 + 2 = 9 and 9 + 3 = 12. Attach our apartment number and you get 126.
- The first day of summer is June 21, 6-21 representing the sun. 621 reversed is 126.
- After my operation following the shooting, the first thing that came into focus after the anesthesia slowly wore off was my room number, 126.
- Pat Porter, the mother of my first child, was born on 6/12 (126).
- My first child's name is Lorrell Faison. L is the twelfth letter of the alphabet, and F is the sixth letter—126.
- When I visited the Roc-A-Fella records office to do business about the film, I noticed the office suite number was 126.

Game Over

- J is the 10th letter of the alphabet, and Z is the 26th letter—126.
- When I read *The Autobiography of Malcolm X*, I noticed a chapter called "Trapped," which I eventually made the title of my screenplay about my life. That chapter summed up all my feelings about growing up in Harlem and becoming a drug dealer. That chapter began on page 126.
- Michelle was the mother of my daughter Azzia. She lived on 126th Street. I always used the code 126 to page her.
- I remember reading a poster advertising the first Million Man March led by Minister Louis Farrakhan and the Nation of Islam. The poster included a verse from the Bible: Genesis 1:26, "Let us make man." I made sure to attend the march.
- The birth of Christ is recorded in the Bible in Luke 1:26.

One day I was in the house by myself when I heard the voice of God. All the "126" stuff had me puzzled, but at that moment it felt like I was in contact with a Divine line. The voice said, "Pick up a pen and do the math. Multiply 360 by the age you will be in the year 2000." That number was 35. When I did the math I came up with 12,600—126 again. Wow. I asked, "Why 360?" The voice said, "360° completes a circle, not 365°." Divine order.

I take strong pride in my relationship with God. My God is the father of all worlds. He speaks to all but we do not listen. Look throughout history. Do the math and you will see that this is true.

Epilogue

The Sun Still Shines

These days I spend my time reading car magazines and going to car shows. I chill with my God, attend movies and plays, and listen to relaxing music. I love spending time with my children. I try my best to teach my children right from wrong and to use my life as an example. There are still demons I have to fight, but at least I'm fighting them. Some people just surrender to their demons or make excuses for them.

When it comes to the drug game, I can honestly say, "Been there, done that." I probably blew more money before I was twenty years old than most people will make in their lifetimes. I shipped enough coke in my past to make it snow in New York City. As a result, I got to live like a ghetto king. Cocaine took me from welfare to well-off in the blink of an eye. I, and thousands of poor young brothers from Harlem, used our wits to outsmart cops and live like the rich bastards we saw on television.

Cats with elementary and high school educations, from broken homes and "at-risk" neighborhoods, became self-made millionaires. The payoffs were unbelievable! Many of us in the game drove some of the hottest cars, rocked some of the most expensive jewelry, and dealt with some of the finest women you've ever seen.

Obviously, there were many downsides to my selling coke. I can honestly say the negatives of the game outweighed the positives: paranoia, lack of sleep, distrust and betrayal, murder and incarceration. I've seen friends kill best friends and uncles kill nephews. I've seen people snitch on their so-called friends to shave some years off their jail sentences. I've experienced some of the greatest tragedies in the 'hood, including the attempt on my life in 1987, the murder of my man Rich, and the kidnapping and murder of his innocent little brother, Donnell William Porter.

As for me personally, I really understand that Langston Hughes poem in which he writes, "Life for me ain't been no crystal stair." I barely escaped a fire that destroyed my entire building as a child. I grew up on welfare. I dropped out in the ninth grade. I got down with the coke game and was able to floss a little bit. During those days, I did so much to violate God's laws that I get a chill just thinking about it.

This is how I know that God is good. Despite those obstacles, despite the poison I sold and the negative energy I supported, God didn't give up on me. In fact, He used my life as a testimony. How else can you explain a former drug dealer starting a rap group, creating a documentary, writing a movie, and publishing a book that teaches people not to do what he did? If that is not God's hand at work, I don't know what is.

God used me, a former hustler, to warn others about the traps called heroin and cocaine. Who else could He use to deliver the message about the drug game, other than a brother who came up through it? The message is clear: A person chooses which road he or she will take in life. With those decisions come consequences, some good and some bad. Very bad choices result in very bad consequences. Sometimes those consequences seem so bad that life begins to lose meaning. The good news is that we always have the chance to listen to God's voice. We can still experience happiness and success no matter what we've done in the past.

The sunrise (God) marks the beginning of a new day. It may rain or snow hard tonight, but the sun still shines tomorrow. With God's help, my light has not gone out. As long as I have breath, I have opportunities to continue exposing the drug game for what it is—a trap. As long as I live, I can help youth see beyond the petty bullshit on their block; I can challenge hip-hop artists to make beautiful music that inspires and teaches truth; I can point people to God's way. Many people were not so lucky.

These days, the huge selection of cars is gone. The jewelry, huge houses, and "down-for-whateva" hoes are gone. The stash houses full of money are gone. People in my neighborhood might recognize me and think that I went from rich to poor. They might think I "fell off." They've got it twisted.

I'm actually wealthier now than I was when I sold cocaine. I'm more on point than ever these days because I know who I am and why I am. The world is very wicked today, and many people are lost. But as far as I can tell, the *sun* still shines. And every time I see the sun, I see God, and I see myself. Despite all the clouds in my life, despite all the storms and the pain, I am blessed. I'm God's son. And His *son* still shines.

I was fortunate enough (through the grace of God) to survive the drug game and turn my life around. Many people who get down with the drug game are not as fortunate. Some people did not survive the trap. If everyone reading this book wrote down the names of people we know who were killed or locked up due to drugs, the names would probably cover the Great Wall of China. These names represent millions of lives wasted by the chemical and physical weapons of man.

My community in Harlem and communities all throughout this nation and this world have suffered from the drug game—not just the drugs and the violence of the drug dealers but the corruption of all the law enforcement officials and politicians who benefit from the sale of narcotics. One day I wrote down the names of all my friends and people I knew who got killed in the drug game. The list brings tears to my eyes whenever I see it:

- Donnell William Porter
- Donald "L.A." Johnson

The Sun Still Shines

- Tee Money
- Mike
- Jason
- Wild Al
- Rashid
- Travis
- Jamaican Mikey
- Kato
- Will 145
- Red 132
- Peter Rabbit
- Charles Johnson
- Ras Clad
- Big Anthony-B
- Baby J Harris
- John John
- Vaughn Drew
- Ms. Chiles
- Myra Enoch
- Joanne Blue
- Shameeka
- Elaine 134
- Big L
- Wolf
- Dondie
- Champ
- Clyde
- Benny Hampton
- Blue
- Cockoo

Game Over

- Chip Banks
- Carlton Hines
- Black Just
- 50 Cent Brooklyn
- LuLu
- Tom Low
- Jamaican Pree
- Frank Nitty
- Montana
- Lil Po
- Jermaine
- Hen Dog
- Nappy Red
- Lil Scotty
- Bracie
- Jamie-O
- G Man
- Dog Food
- Drag O
- Brother Charles X
- D Ferg
- Pork Chop
- Bro Chicken Wing
- Shaft
- Thomas Mapper
- Allen Lloyd
- Small Paul
- Mr. Vincent
- Paris
- Pepsi Daryl

The Sun Still Shines

- Fat Country
- Big Dave Gusto
- Kev Campbell
- Nadine
- LTD
- Curt
- Tye Buddy
- Ali-Moe
- Marlon
- Elton 146
- Don B
- Lil Boo
- 46 the Cabdriver
- Smiley
- Keith
- Buzz
- Jamaican Bird
- BT Boston
- Renee Boston
- Charlie Kimball
- Frank Kimball
- Johnny Kimball
- Fat Jeff
- Mickey Brown
- Stanley Harvey
- Maximo
- Shawn Moe
- Fritz
- Steve Ash
- Scoosie

- Butter
- Lil Tone
- Wrinkle
- Butch
- Boost
- Tone Hood
- Richard Porter
- Tony Scott
- Joe Cherry
- Lowell Hill
- Mr. Wilson
- Phoenix
- Eighty-Eight
- Craig
- Felicia
- Elliott
- Sheisty
- Big Dave
- Baron Beasley

Think of all the families destroyed by their deaths. Think of all the good police officers and other law enforcement officials who were also casualties of the drug war. Think of all the innocent people accidentally killed by drug dealers or cops chasing them. Do you think cars, sex, and property is worth all the death and destruction that follows? Think again.

To all the brothers and sisters selling drugs or using drugs . . . to all the rap artists who glorify the drug game . . . to all the cops who accept bribes from drug dealers . . . to all the lawyers and judges who profit from narcotics . . . to all the parents or loved ones of drug dealers who accept their money and gifts, please *feel* what I'm about to say. I've dumped my brain into this book, sharing with complete strangers all the details of my life. Exposing my past mistakes and sins was not easy, in fact, it was painful and sometimes embarrassing to expose these things.

I shared every opinion and experience out of love and sincerity. I sold drugs myself, so I do not stand in judgment of any hustlers. My goal is not to bark on people or point fingers at anyone. If anything, I more than anyone understand why people sell and use drugs. I sold drugs at the highest level, so I know what I'm talking about. I realize that poverty and lack of education and job skills steer cats to sell narcotics. Pain, self-hatred, and lack of support make people use drugs to escape the pain they suffer. Despite all of this, we still have the power to choose. You read about the choices I made, and the choices of my associates. You also saw the consequences of these decisions.

These stories are not from a Hollywood movie script or street novel. These are all true stories. I didn't share my story to entertain you or brag about my past. I don't want to be remembered as the "Harlem kingpin." All the craziness I went through means nothing if I don't help other people to see the light. I don't claim to have all the answers or solutions. I just want people to stop howling at the moon (money) like wolves, and begin turning to the sun (God's way). Wise people can make the right decisions by learning from the mistakes of others. We can learn from our mistakes and choose a different path.

Cocaine, heroin, angel dust, and other narcotics served their purpose: to make our communities weak, prevent the possibility of social justice, and relocate *undesirable* people to prisons, crazy houses, and graveyards. Why? So *desirable* people can relocate into former slums. Why do you think our governing bodies create "empowerment zones" and "urban renewal" programs? Do the math!

The drug game will never be the same. Drug and gun laws are stronger, jail sentences are longer, and the cops are equipped with more weapons and technology. People may try to glamorize the drug game, but they don't tell you about the stiff jail sentences awaiting those convicted of selling crack. The Rockefeller Drug Law, for example, makes convicted dealers serve a mandatory sentence of *fifteen years to life* for selling *two ounces or possessing four ounces of a narcotic.* In addition, the police can also take a drug dealer's home, property, or legitimate businesses.

Don't believe the hype! Most young brothers slinging coke, crack, or heroin will not see the type of money Rich, Alpo, and I saw back in the days. Times were different then. These days, you have a better chance by getting an education, getting into the music game, or starting a legitimate business than you do by selling drugs. Today there are more hustlers than customers! Stricter laws, snitches, and surveillance make it almost impossible today to hustle without getting caught.

Clearly, the drug game leads to death, destruction, and incarceration. My life bears witness to this statement, as do the lives of everyone I listed a few pages back. It is God's way or the highway. This past is history, and the future is a mystery. You don't go to Heaven, you grow to Heaven. "Let he who has not sinned cast the first stone." The sun still shines forever . . . Game over.

126—PEACE

Acknowledgments

To the Lord of the entire world—the central sun!

Thank You for giving life to all. Without You there is none. If I knew then what I know now, I would never have run.

To All the Great Men and Women
Who Help Us to See Again

THE LORD JESUS, Moses, ATTETON, 126 my FATHER AZIE FAISON, aka "ACE THE REAL AZ," Malcolm X, Martin Luther King Jr., Alex Haley, John F. Kennedy, Bob Marley, Bruce Lee, Muhammad Ali, Big Ice, Gandhi, Master Farad Mohammed, Elijah Muhammad, Minister Farrakhan and the Nation of Islam, Bishop T. D. Jakes, Mustafa 149, Belinda Womack, Rakim, Chuck D and Public Enemy, KRS-One, Tupac Shakur, Nas, OutKast, David Ikey, Dr. Valentine, Dr. Malachi York and the Ansaar family, Peter Gabriel, Phil Collins, John Lennon, Pink Floyd, REM, Coldplay, Marvin Gaye, Steve Arrington, Ray Charles, Stevie Wonder, Curtis Mayfield, James Brown, Barry White, the Isley Brothers, Isaac Hayes, Harold

Acknowledgments

Melvin & the Blue Notes, Donny Hathaway, Sam Cooke, Melba Moore, Tina Marie, Diana Ross, Gladys Knight, George Clinton, Bootsy Collins, DMD, Pearl Jam, Genesis, Sade, Donnie McClurkin, Patti LaBelle, Aretha Franklin, Stephanie Mills, Angela Bofill, the Winans, Earth Wind & Fire, the Jacksons, New Edition, Bobby and Whitney, Run DMC, LL Cool J, Jay-Z, Melle Mel, Ice Cube, Dr. Dre, Snoop Dogg, Janet Jackson, Jim Brown, John Amos, Kool & the Gang, Charlie Wilson, R. Kelly, Lionel Richie, the Temptations, Miles Davis, Howard Hewitt, Blue Magic, Barbra Streisand, Elvis Presley, Michael Jackson, Richard Pryor, Steve Harvey, Russell Simmons, Eddie Murphy, Redd Foxx, Maya Angelou, Ossie Davis, Ruby Dee, Pam Grier, Halle Berry, Danny Glover, the Wayans brothers, Jim Kelly, Calvin Lockhart, Sidney Poitier, Harry Belafonte, Bill Cosby, Morgan Freeman, Mary Nell, Billie Holiday, Cab Calloway, Louis Armstrong, Nat "King" Cole, Sammy Davis, Jr., Erykah Badu, Prince, India.Arie, Arthur Ashe, Bill Russell, Michael Jordan, Magic Johnson, Larry Bird, Pistol Pete Maravich, Kareem Abdul-Jabbar, Roberto Clemente, Reggie Jackson, Hank Aaron, Jackie Robinson, Babe Ruth, Denzel Washington, Oprah Winfrey, Robert Johnson and BET, Rosa Parks, Spike Lee, Colin Powell, Johnnie Cochran, Councilman James E. Davis, Edgar Casey, Dr. Betty Shabazz, Coretta Scott King, Mark Tillinger, and the Guardian Angels. All of Harlem, Rich, Donnell and the Porter family, Lincoln and Mt. Sinai Hospitals for saving my life, Lynette Bell, Michael Lamar and Joanne Blue, Coffee, Alpo, MobStyle, *F.E.D.S.* magazine, *Don Diva*, StreetStar Inc., *Vibe*, and *The Source* magazines, everyone involved with the *Game Over* documentary and the movie *Paid in Full*, Young Jeezy, Akon, Cam'Ron, Dr. Wayne Dyer, Pop from Blackstar, Artists Only Records, Mr. Ed and Rick at DubItAll, Jos 66, Mark H. and family 53, Jack Goldberg, Tim Dog (Butt Naked Entertainment), Reverend Craig Ward, the Gant family, Busy Bee, Angela in Poughkeepsie, Sheila Lindsay (my crutch), Shannon ("Let the

Acknowledgments

Music Play"), Erick the Big Apple, Twin and family, and Harvey Weinstein at Miramax. I am not worthy to walk in the shoes of many of these people I listed. Global warming . . . save yourself! God bless the entire world.

Family

My father, Azie Faison, Sr., my dear mother, Margaret Rogers, Pat and Velma Porter, my firstborn, Lorrel Faison, my but-but, Azzia Faison, Robin and Roselyn Person, Wonda Neeley, Kevin Neeley, Julie Faison, Ingrid Rogers, Wayne Rogers, R. Smith, Berell, Antoine and family, Shelly and family.

Thanks for Your Support

Jerry Holmes, Clayton Simmons, Mr. Ed and Ritchie Rich, Dubitall, Carlton Porter, Troy Reed, Dame Dash, Larry Boston, Godfrey Johnson, Nick Thomas, Big Mike from Queens, Shawn Washington, Sherman, Jody Walker, Jason Lynn, Gerry Walker, Chewie, Jojo White, James Drayton, Lora, Dr. Beat and Control, Jesus (Eye On It), L Gee, Mr. and Ms. Robinson (Sugar Hill Records), Gerry and Danny, Steve (Texas Star Diner), Chris Coleman, Mike and Ed, Blue Star Inc., Matrix Films, Uncle Ralph, Vaughn Mason, and Lance Hayes.

Special Thanks

Judith Curr, Malaika Adero, and Krishan Trotman and all the people from Atria Books; my agent Marie Brown and coauthor Agyei Tyehimba. Thanks to all of you for giving me the opportunity to tell my story.

Agyei's Acknowledgments

To brother Azie for agreeing to work with me to tell his story in book form. Make them bear witness, A! To Marie Brown, my agent and former teacher, for believing in the project, and keeping us on task. To Simon & Schuster/Atria Books for having the vision and faith to publish a street story that transcends the streets. To friends and family who were very supportive throughout the process of writing this book: my cousin Illona Jones, Kamau M'Bhaso, Dr. James Turner at Cornell University, Dr. Scot Brown at UCLA, Johnny Velasquez, Marcus Gates, "D-Murda" (freedom and respect over money), the Gant family, Cheryl Wills, Bernice Risbrook, and Reggie and Theresa Mays. Beloved family members passed on during the making of this book. It hurts to know they are not here to see the fruits of our labor. I pray that this work honors their legacy: my father, George W. Stith (my first hero), my grandmother Oleathia Stith, and my aunt Janice Frederick. May you all rest in peace . . .